# TRANSITION

# TRANSITION

MOFFAT DAVID

Mireads

# Contents

*Dedication* viii

*Transition* 1

FOREWORD

PROLOGUE

1 Transition, what it is 7

2 Transition, why talk about it? 17

3 Transition, its purpose 25

4 Transition, it's God's prerogative! 33

5 Transition, how it happens 53

6 Premature transition 71

7 Transition and transmission 83

8 Honoring those who transition 93

9 Mourning those who transition 103

10 Raw emotion and allowing to be comforted 116

11 How to receive God's comfort 129

12 Helping children with loss 138

13 Transition minded 155
14 Seeing transition through the lens of God's love 176
15 The door to heaven 186
References 188
*About The Author* 191

First Printing, 2021

*Dedication*

*Sean and Aretha*
*'May you never despair with a divine transition!'*

*Debbie.*
*'forever cherished ...'*

# Transition

*change*

*transformation*

*conversion*

*adaptation*

*changeover*

*metamorphosis*

*shift*

*switch*

*jump*

*leap*

*progress*

*transfiguration*

*mutation*

*transmutation*

# Foreword

There are many books that have been written on the subject of death and dying. There are equally numerous doctrinal discussions concerning the afterlife. Any careful student of scriptures understands the Christian belief concerning death: in essence, the gospel declares the victory of Jesus Christ over death and the grave. Christians believe that because Jesus Christ died and rose from the grave, everyone who believes in Him shall also be raised from the dead upon the Lord's return.

However, a misinterpretation of this fundamental Christian tenet has led to a pervasive failure of the church to offer an appropriate response to the experience of death and the sorrow which those left behind undergo. In other words, since Christians believe that everyone who dies in faith shall be raised from the grave, how do we grieve their loss? Are Christians even allowed to grieve? Does the hope of the resurrection of the dead remove the need for grief in Christians?

In a very vulnerable and highly reflective narrative Moffat has offered some insights from a deeply personal experience as well as a comprehensive theological perspective. The depth of the teaching as well as the richness of the emotional energy infused into the wisdom shared in these pages is guaranteed to comfort the heart of anyone who has experienced grief and loss either recently or in the distant past. The personal pain which the author has experienced several times, over qualifies him more than many others to speak so authoritatively on these very delicate issues which affect every person, Christian or not.

This book is equipped to empower anyone with a keen desire to grow in how they process grief from a sound doctrinal basis. In these pages the word finds expression in reality which embraces with compassion the bleeding heart of every grieving soul.


Justice Dr. Chifundo Jairus Kachale

***Chairperson***

***Malawi Electoral Commission***

***(2020 to 2024)***

***Malawi High Court Judge***

# Prologue

Transition is a book I never thought I would write. A book I was very reluctant to write, but one that I felt necessary to write. A direct sequel to 'Supernatural Homecomings' another book I was almost forced to write due to my curiosity about loss and, almost as a direct way of dealing with the loss of my sister Danielle in November 2016.

As life would have it this loss was just the beginning of sorrows and daggers that would continue to pierce my heart. Barely 3 years later in October 2019 I would lose yet someone else so close to me, my dear wife Debbie of 10 years just a month after our 10th wedding anniversary. The pain was unforgiving, the sorrow heart wrenching,... and barely 9 months later, our family would lose our Dad in June 2020, just as I was about to finish this book. This loss was painful in its own way, our flame of hope for his recovery flared in hope, then flickered in despair and died in trauma. But through it all, I got a vision from God, a vision through his word alone, that, 'we don't actually die, we simply transition!'

Many don't have to deal with the pain of loss for a while, but, as life 'happens', it becomes a reality for many of us, and whether curious or afraid we come to a place we can only describe as being 'between a rock and hard place'. My prayer is that through the revelations in this book, as I was strengthened, they may equally be encouraged, strengthened and perhaps that they don't despair, once they understand that a divine 'transition' has taken place!

*Your ability to deal with deep pain and loss is not dependent on your age or the number of funerals you have attended, it's not based on what you do in life whether as a leader in matters of faith or in the marketplace. It's based, only, on what God reveals to you! And on the truth of God's word. Everything else is shockingly and pathetically inadequate, regardless of how well equipped we think we are.*

Many have literally broken down emotionally, spiritually and mentally and have become a mere shadow of their former selves. Those affected include, both male and female, macho men in particular, naturally resilient women, young and old, nobles and paupers, and sadly, pastors and ordinary believers alike, in other words both the shepherd and the sheep are scattered by this ravaging predator if they remain blind to the truth of God's word.

This is not God's will for his children. He wants us to have a true and pure revelation of what death is and how he is our strength and fortress in times of deep loss and pain.

Moffat David
*FCCA, CA(Mw) (CGEIT), B Acc.*

# I

# Transition, what it is

Transition has many synonyms such as

*"Change, move, passage, transformation, conversion, adaptation, alteration, changeover, metamorphosis, shift, switch"*

*"Jump, leap, progression, progress, gradation, development, transfiguration, flux, mutation, transmutation"*

I would love to describe each of these rich words but let me simply describe transition as

*'The act of passing from one state or place to the next'*

*'An event that results in a transformation'*

*'A change from one place, state, subject or stage or another'*

The truth of the matter is that man is a spirit who lives in a body and who interacts with this world through his soul or mind. This spirit is described as the true 'essence' of a person and is a considered as the seat of emotions and character. It is the true self! The soul is the consciousness while the spirit is a different dimension of man. The soul is conscious of its surroundings through its body. It is the seat of the spirit, the true you, and through the soul, the spirit interacts with the world.

The spirit shows it's true colors through the manifestation of different emotions and character.

Modern science remains intrigued with this concept of a 'spirit' so much so that the idea of consciousness after death, and the connection of mind and consciousness remains a matter of scientific research to this day. Science describes what is called a 'near death experience' or NDE. It is a phenomenon that is studied the world over and it pertains to personal experiences of people near to, or at the point of death. It has even been researched that the spirit of a man, also called the 'soul', 'consciousness' or 'the psyche' has a weight! Dr Duncan McDougall researched that the human body loses about 21 grams of weight at the point of death ("Weight of the soul" by Mikkelson, Barbara). One consistent fact is now being established that people who have had NDE's were fully conscious of their surroundings and events around their death even while they were pronounced clinically dead!

Researchers at NYU have also established that consciousness goes beyond the point of death, once a person is pronounced clinically deceased, even though there is no medical reason for this to be the case.

What scientists are discovering today is not new to the Bible. In fact the Bible speaks a lot about death but we just don't see it. And naturally so! ... we shy away from and steer clear of this topic of course! The Bible says that as opposed to an evolution theory or the Big Bang theory there was a process of creation and that in this process, man was created, and that God breathed life into Adam, and he became a living soul.

Once the body dies, the spirit has no need for a body to interact with this physical world. The real you or the real essence then shifts into another dimension!

### *Transition, calling death what it is*

All the words that describe death have naturally been affected by our experiences. The word death itself implies '*lifelessness*', and '*the end of all things and of our consciousness*'. In my culture a death is described as 'a mourning' or 'a loss'. In one African language called 'chichewa' words such as 'munthu wamwalira' literally and *crudely* translated is a combination of two words which mean ***'someone has... you have cried'*** which means 'Someone has made you cry'. It means 'someone has died' and therefore 'you have cried' and 'you have mourned'.

So, as in other languages and cultures around the world, most definitions of death are associated with loss or experiences to do with the finality of this life, and the finality of 'consciousnesses'. The English word 'death' itself is a reminder of this finality. Death, as we know it in human terms, is described as 'a permanent end to all life functions' or 'the absence of life' or 'the end of life'. And it has other names such as 'loss' which emphasize feelings of emptiness. But the Bible has several descriptions of the very same concept which paint a totally different picture!

### *Homecoming*

One of the perceptions I personally like is the description of a homecoming. Jesus takes time to explain our future home by saying '*In fact I am going to prepare a place for you because in my father's house are many rooms and mansions. Where I will be you will be also and I will come to take you to where I am' (John 14:6).*

So Jesus is saying *'heaven is our father's house'*. And when I read this in view of what he says next, I have come to the almost certain and logical conclusion that he is not just talking of one physical house with many rooms... no he is talking of house in the sense of a 'family line' or 'lineage' such as the 'The House of York' for example. Jesus is saying 'the father's house and family line has many rooms and mansions.' It's not just one house with a hotel like structure that has many rooms! Not at all it's a house of families or group of families that have many houses. When I think of this I think of an African rural village in which all the family members build houses next to each other and they end up mushrooming into a whole community and neighborhood.

The houses in heaven, however, are a reflection the type of person inhabiting it, the achievements of the person and the reward that God is giving to them as his sons and daughters. Those who have been blessed enough to see visions of heaven or to be taken to heaven for brief visions and visits describe beautiful homes for God's people. In Africa the concept of house can be easier to understand because when I go to an African village, I realize that there are many houses in one village which are arranged or naturally clustered according to families. The clusters will be named by the family that occupies it, and the well being of each family is known by the type of development or houses they have.

In 'God's House' the *'House of Jehovah'* or the *'House of Yeshua'* there are many rooms, beautiful houses and mansions that are freely available for its heirs.

Jesus is therefore saying 'life on earth is not permanent because you have a home!' He says 'there will be a homecoming one day!' He even adds to this and says 'I will come and take you! So I may share the pleasures of my father's house with you! Where I am you will be also. I want to share my father's house with you!'

## *Putting off the tent*

Apostle Paul has a great concept of what death really is.

He said we have two types of dwelling. One is heavenly and one is earthly. The earthly is a tent and is destroyed but we have another tent that is not built with hands but that is eternal and is heavenly!

A tent has never been called a house. It is temporal in nature, in fact it is a 'portable house' that you carry along with you. You keep it in shape and good condition. You take care of it because you need it for a harsh night out in the cold or in the wind, high in the mountains or deep in the woods. You may even cook a meal in it but it's function is really limited. It may not be something you would live permanently in unless you are really homeless. That's what our bodies are, they are a tent for temporary use and a shelter on this camping trip of life. Afterwards we go to our real home. The one Jesus calls 'My Father's House' and in which are many mansions.

This home is permanent and heavenly and is a heavenly body that is as glorious as the body of Jesus Christ. It is a resurrection body that will one day be given to us. This body has no limitations and is indestructible. Like the body of Jesus our spiritual body can appear and disappear it can move through walls and travel at the speed of light. It is a glorious body and this earthly body pales in comparison!

That's why Paul says while I am in this limited body... I groan for something more permanent and more glorious! He says

*'For in this tent we groan, longing to put on our heavenly dwelling'* 2 *Corinthians 5:2.*

So for a true christian death is the laying aside of this earthly tent after it serves its purpose of providing temporary and well needed shelter from the harsh element of what we call life!

*'... I know that the putting off of my body will be soon...'*

*2 Peter 1:14.*

### *Entering a door*

In my book supernatural 'homecomings' I captured many stories of what people experienced or said they were experiencing as they passed on. One of the most common things was the fact that many of them said they saw a door. They would say 'My door is open' 'my time is up'. 'I am going'.

A door is a means of access through which you enter or leave a room or building. It is also a barrier that prevents access into another room. Death is like that. As we transition a door is actually opened into another world. The spiritual, eternal and more permanent world that exists after this life!

For a christian, he need not fear or despair regarding death. I mostly wonder what the dying experience and think of, before dying. I know that those who do not believe in Christ have experiences of darkness fear and dread. But believers are blessed with something unique. They have a blessing because they have Jesus in their hearts.

Why is Jesus important in death! It's because he is the very means of our conveyance into heaven! In John 10:7 He declares, that I am the door into heaven by saying

*"Truly, truly, I say to you, I am the door of the sheep"*

In fact he starts from verse 1 of this chapter saying he is also the shepherd of the sheep. One unique thing about his shepherding role is the fact that he talks to his sheep and that his sheep hear his voice. This is particularly important in the Christian's transition because at the point of transition Jesus is actually in control and actually calls out to his sheep. Yes, when it is time, he bids them 'Come'.

Once his sheep hear his voice, the spirit of the believer recognizes the Shepherds voice and naturally obeys.

*'and the sheep hear his voice: and he calleth his own sheep by name, and leadeth them out.' John 10:3*

In fact in 1 Peter 2:25 Jesus is described as the shepherd and overseer, and guardian and bishop of our very souls. Therefore with such a powerful role, Jesus is with us at every step of the way in the process of transition or what we fearfully call death.

*"and lo, I am with you always [remaining with you perpetually—regardless of circumstance (this does not exclude death), and on every occasion], even to the end of the age." Matthew 28:20 AMP*

Look at it this way... Jesus is effectively saying 'I will never leave you nor forsake you' 'not even in the moment of death or even to the end of your time or age on earth'.

I always imagine how families gather to welcome or bid each other farewell on momentous occasions. Especially when families travel. I recall when I was first put on a coach traveling about 900km away to boarding school. My mum and dad would always take me to the bus, ensure I am well taken care of by the hostess and then be safely sent on my way. My mum would be teary eyed of course, as most mothers usually are. I recall the same scenario almost 20 years later when one of her nieces called Hillary was going for university studies in China. This time a bus was not involved and she was leaving by plane and those that surrounded her were family. We took pictures and hugged and laughed and lo and behold my mum was just as teary eyed as ever before. We all laughed at her and said 'grand ma she is just leaving for school'. The scenario was exactly the same when my brother Joshua went to pursue his masters Degree in Australia. He was surrounded by family and one teary mum. On his return however there were no tears, only crocodile smiles from my mum. Well..., if truth be told, she might have shed a tear or two but it was certainly a tear of joy!

When my brother's family was relocating to South Africa the scenario was the same, surrounded by family and a teary eyed mom. What is the point of all this? The point is 'Jesus is our family'. He is called 'our brother'. The other point is this, 'where you are going you are always accompanied or welcomed by family!' In fact transition is a homecoming to your family!

When Christians transition they are in principle welcomed by Jesus and the Father. They are coming home and when making this great relocation of life this heavenly family surrounds them. That's why Jesus talks of 'my father's house' and 'where I will be you will be also' and he says 'I go to prepare a place for you'.

So be assured of one thing, you are not alone but are also welcomed by your brother Jesus and your Father in heaven! So about death Jesus declares

*'Don't stress my child! Transition is my business as the bishop, guardian and overseer of your soul! I am with you all the way. In fact you are never alone in your transition and you are simply coming home.'*

In my book Supernatural homecomings there is a true story of, a great musician of our time who at the age of 4 fell from the 4th floor of a building. He was pronounced dead on the spot and was welcomed by Jesus. However Jesus gave him a choice to go with him or stay on earth. Jesus asked him *'do you want to go home with me or do you want to stay with your mom'*.

What you will notice is that Jesus is measured and deliberate in his words. He calls heaven as 'home' but not so his 'moms house'! He simply says do you want to go to your mum! This is a powerful revelation that heaven is your home! Your earthly dwelling place is just a temporary arrangement. While camping through life you are given a tent to hide in. If you choose to create a bunker it is still just that 'a bunker' and not a home.

I also believe, based on the Bible, that in heaven our earthly family of believers who have died will definitely welcome us and rejoice at our coming home! There are several examples of this in the Bible.

On the mount of transfiguration we see that Jesus interacted with Moses and Elijah and in the story of Lazarus and the rich man we see that the spirit of Abraham received and comforted the soul of Lazarus!

I have also heard of a story of a missionary who while dying confessed *'I can see Jesus and my husband smiling at me!'* This means if your loved ones were saved and died before us, we will see them in heaven in fact they will even welcome us!

So, on our transition we meet up with our loved ones in heaven. In fact they long to see you again!

Another example of this is a story in my book supernatural homecomings of a lady named Sarah. God announced her homecoming in a vision and a trance and it was clear that a homecoming celebration was being planned in heaven!

This was revealed to the co-pastor of Sarah, McDonald, and the words in the vision that occurred about two or three times were 'my servant is coming home,' and with these words was as vision of an elaborate celebration that was being planned in heaven!

So death is a transition and not just a transition but more so, a happy and celebratory homecoming!

### *Returning our breath to God*

Transition is also a returning of the breath that comes from God, the author of life. Our lives will be called upon at some point in time when the time is right.

When God created Adam the Bible says he breathed life into him and this breath of life is not our own.

*'and the dust returns to the earth as it was, and the spirit returns to God who gave it.' Ecclesiastes 12:7*

I recall the biblical story of a rich man who had a great harvest and had grand plans for himself. God called him a fool and said '*I will demand your life this very night!*' (Luke 12:20). And in Psalms 146:4 the Bible says '*when his breath departs, he returns to the earth; on that very day his plans perish*'.

I have always wondered what this verse means especially in regard to the tripartite nature of man. Man is a spirit, he has a body and also a mind that is used to think and interact with his surroundings. The mind is the result of the fusion of the spirit and the body. This talk, of the spirit going back to its maker, triggers a few questions,

'*Is this returning to a permanent position in heaven regardless of our deeds?*
'So do all spirits, good and bad still end up in heaven?

As far as I know the rest of the Bible does not support this argument. What seems plausible is that this is the normal sequence of events or the journey that all human spirits normally take. All spirits must stand before God for accountability!

'*And as it is appointed unto men once to die, but after this the judgment' Hebrews 9:27*

'*For we must all appear before the judgment seat of Christ; that every one may receive the things done in his body, according to that he hath done, whether it be good or bad.' 2 Corinthians 5:10*

After we appear before God we are then sent to our final destinations of eternal life or eternal punishment.

Another thing this means is that we are not in control of our lives! Whenever God demands or calls back his spirit in us we will surely transition!

This also emphasizes the fact that we are not our own and that our life is simply a gift. Life was simply given and breathed into us as he 'formed Adam, breathed into him and he became a living soul!'

*"You turn man back to dust, And say, "Return [to the earth], O children of [mortal] men!"" Psalms 90:3 AMP*

### *Sleeping*

Death is also called sleeping. The term has been used since the Old Testament times. For example David is said to have slept with his fathers and the Old Testament has a total of 36 repetitions of this phrase made for various Kings and people including King David and King Solomon.

Jesus said the little girl who died was simply sleeping and not dead. Jesus even set off to Lazarus' house only after Lazarus died and said 'our friend Lazarus is sleeping' (1 Kings 2:10, Lk 8:52, Jn 11:11).

The main thing we get from this phrase is that we always wake up from sleep and that death is not permanent. It is a temporary state in our eternal journey. We will be resurrected to the resurrection of life or to the resurrection of judgement and damnation. So, contrary to the public opinion of finality, death is temporary and only a stage in our eternal journeys.

*Behold, I shew you a mystery; We shall not all sleep, but we shall all be changed, In a moment, in the twinkling of an eye, at the last trump: for the trumpet shall sound, and the dead shall be raised incorruptible, and we shall be changed. 1 Corinthians 15:51-52*

*For the Lord himself shall descend from heaven with a shout, with the voice of the archangel, and with the trump of God: and the dead in Christ shall rise first: Then we which are alive and remain shall be caught up together with them in the clouds, to meet the Lord in the air: and so shall we ever be with the Lord.*

*1 Thessalonians 4:16-17*

# 2

# Transition, why talk about it?

Transition or death is something we normally don't talk about. But there are several reasons why we must! Practically death brings a lot of changes and adjustments to life that are unexpected and for which we are naturally unprepared! As a result it's impact is so significant on many fronts. It is said that things that have the most significant impact on people's life are death and divorce and breakups of serious relationships.

### *It is wise to think about death*

*"A wise person thinks a lot about death, while a fool thinks only about having a good time." Ecclesiastes 7:4 NLT*

God does not want us to ignore the inevitable. He told Adam that he will die and return to the dust of the earth so naturally death is unavoidable.

When you are dealing with the inevitable, we can't bury our heads in the sand and do nothing about it. No! we must prepare for it.

## *Death happens to all*

*There is a time for everything. There is a time to be born and a time to die.. (Eccl 3:3)*

This is a set principle of nature and this is common to all. The preacher, in Ecclesiastes, in fact hopes that this would not be the case but alas he saw a tragedy that affects all men rich and poor, good and bad alike!

*All share a common destiny—the righteous and the wicked, the good and the bad, the clean and the unclean, those who offer sacrifices and those who do not.*

*As it is with the good,*
*so with the sinful;*
*as it is with those who take oaths,*
*so with those who are afraid to take them.*

*This is the evil in everything that happens under the sun: The same destiny overtakes all. The hearts of people, moreover, are full of evil and there is madness in their hearts while they live,* ***and afterward they join the dead****. Ecclesiastes 9:2-3*

## *Death is difficult to deal with*

The fact that death is a truly a natural part of human existence has certainly not made it easier to deal with. Death is something we all want to avoid talking about, let alone experience it for ourselves!

Death is something we don't fully understand until it has affected you closely and personally. It is also very unexpected by its nature and I feel we become the best comforters when we either have a sober and mature mindset or if we have personally experienced it when it robs us of our loved ones.

Most people crumble inside under the pressure of the sheer pain they experience. It's something totally human or natural but also totally unexpected. It is something in which we do not get training on how to respond to and yet we must deal with it when it comes and affects our loved ones. This challenge makes others cope better than some. That which makes them cope can be called many things, but for now I think it's called hope, and it's called faith, and this is a faith in God and his word!

### *Death challenges our theology*

If Christianity cannot conquer death we have no point being Christians at all. I say this because death forces us to critically examine what we believe in sincerity or choose to believe in naivety.

When you apply your mind to it you will realize that what God is promising Christians is truly mind boggling. Mind boggling in the sense that the promise of life after death is not something we can prove. But also it's mind boggling because we can't understand the immense power that is required for a resurrection of the body as preached by Christ and as taught by the Bible.

At the point of death you question your theology you ask several questions such as

*'Is there really life after death?*

*Is my loved one really alive?*

*Is my loved one in heaven or in hell?*

*Will this decomposing body really be recreated and resurrected again on earth?*

Now... these are difficult questions! The answer to these questions applies to us because we too shall die. So we too ask ourselves,

*'When I die what will happen to me?*

*Will I live on?*

*Will I enter heaven?*

*Will I miss heaven for hell?*

*Will this decomposing body really be recreated and resurrected again on earth?*

Friends when faced with questions like these you need a solid faith! You need a solid redeemer and you need a living and almighty God!

It's no longer about taking 1 day or 2 hours of your week to attend prayer or to simply belong and be accepted in a grouping of people. It's about you! It's personal! It's about where you will be when you take your last breath. It's about being truly alive in the inside of you and existing after this life!

You see, if there is no resurrection or life after death we are the most pitied of faiths. Why? Because life after death and resurrection is not simply a *bold* thing to believe in. It is an *audacious* thing to believe in! It requires a power so high and so mighty that it is able to create and restore and recreate! It requires a power that is in command and truly in control of the universe!

This is a scary thought and believe it or not this is what comes into our minds when we face death. It may not come as clear as presented here, because mostly we suppress those thoughts. But believe you me! We think these thoughts!

Part of our theology is that

*God is love!*

*God is in control!*

*He is a healer!*

*He is all powerful!*

*He is all knowing!*

*He holds the whole world in his hands!*

*He is a deliverer!*

*He answers prayer!*

*He honors and quickly responds to prayer and fasting!*

Well.... let me burst your bubble! When death happens even these beliefs are questioned! Why? Simply because before our loved ones died, ....

'*We trusted in God's love*

*We believed God is in control! And that*

*He is a healer!*

*He is all powerful!*

*He is all knowing!*

*He holds the whole world in his hands!*

*He is a deliverer!*

*He answers prayer!*

*He honors and quickly responds to prayer and fasting!*

This is why death is so difficult to even the most faithful of Christians. Because at this point our theology is seemingly shattered and our hopes are seemingly lost. But this should not be so. I am hoping that like Job we too can realize that

*'God is sovereign*

*God answers no man*

God allows the enemy to seemingly triumph because God does not suffer from the need to punish and judge the enemies of sin and death immediately. God allows the laws of this world to take their natural course! Because of Adam's sin in the Bible sin entered the world. Good people therefore can also be attacked by disease, sin and violence.

When our mindsets are challenged and they eventually give! The enemy puts subtle questions in our minds and asks

*'if God were good how can all this pain and suffering be allowed to happen?'*

This is why we need to talk about death?! To reach out to those who are wounded and traumatized. So they will have hope! So they will know that God is always in control. God allows suffering but even though he allows it, he will ultimately destroy death, sin and all its effects on mankind.

So that when suffering comes, your faith will not be shaken!

## *The day of death is greater than the day of birth*

*"A good name is better than precious perfume, And the day of one's death better than the day of one's birth." Ecclesiastes 7:1 AMP*

The first cry of a child is a joyous moment. The curiosity follows of whether it's a boy or girl and an appropriate name quickly follows. It's the beginning of a life of promise. This little baby can become strong and mighty in the land! Though feeble and fragile this could become a king, a queen, a prince or a princess! This child can be the source of joy and great pride.

This *'day of promise'* however is said to pale in comparison to *'the gift that actually was'*. The day of death is not a day of promise rather it is a day of remembering and cherishing the actual gift that someone has been. It's not about *'what could be'* but about *'what has been!'*

It's a greater day because the day of death is the culmination of all that *'could have been'* into the actual *'has been'*. It is the sum total of the hidden treasure of a day-old baby!

This day is a day of much more significance than birth for it is the moment of truth. It is a day of either great gladness or great sorrow. It is a day of great fulfillment of grand expectations or of disappointment as we ponder what a waste a life has been. This is a greater day! A more solemn day! Not a day of promise but of achievement or lack thereof!

The greatness of this day is not just in witnessing what becomes of our hopes and dreams, no, it has other spiritual importance.

Firstly, it is a day of rest for the believer. Rev 14:13 says this day *'is a day of rest from our labors'*.

*Then I heard a voice from heaven say, "Write this: Blessed are the dead who die in the Lord from now on."*

*"Yes," says the Spirit, "they will rest from their labor, for their deeds will follow them." Revelation 14:13*

The words 'Rest In Peace' are not for everyone! Not at all! According to the word of God they only belong to those who RIP in the Lord Jesus!

If we are not in Jesus by the time we die, then we do not rest but are set for judgement because judgement is our appointment after this life. If our righteousness is not our own and if our righteousness is the righteousness of Jesus and if it is found in the precious blood that was shed for us then we will be acquitted by God and given rest. If not, we face our final judgement and condemnation in eternal punishment for the works we have done in our life!

*'Whether a tree falls to the south or to the north,*
*in the place where it falls, there it will lie.' Ecclesiastes 11:3*

If you die pointing to the north or to heaven, you are heaven bound and will truly Rest In Peace. If you die pointing south or not in the Lord, you are hell bound and cannot Rest In Peace and you are simply waiting for God's final sentencing as you are committed to a place of torment in the interim.

Death brings a sense of deliverance. Deliverance from suffering and grief. We wage fierce wars in life. We wage wars with sickness, tragedies and deep sorrows. We labor and fight these evils throughout our lives, some struggle with and fight excruciating pain that comes from various illnesses but all in all God gives us rest from these labors. So while we want to enjoy the company and presence of our loved ones, sometimes we also appreciate that they have battled long enough, suffered long enough and endured long enough, sometimes we need to accept and let them go to rest from their grief, their pain and their sorrows. So the day of death to them becomes a death to end their suffering and pain and a day of deliverance.

The day of death is also the day of triumph over sin! A day in which the work of sanctification and purification is brought to perfection a day of true deliverance from sin! So that we are tempted no more and we enter into a holy and heavenly world!

The day of death is the day that ushers in a time of heavenly reward.

*How abundant are the good things*
*that you have stored up for those who fear you,*
*that you bestow in the sight of all,*
*on those who take refuge in you. Psalms 31:19*

*However, as it is written:*
*"What no eye has seen, what no ear has heard,*
*and what no human mind has conceived"—*
*the things God has prepared for those who love him—*
*1 Corinthians 2:9*

It is a day in which we await to be enthroned and seated together with Jesus

*To the one who is victorious, I will give the right to sit with me on my throne, just as I was victorious and sat down with my Father on his throne. Revelation 3:21*

It is a day in which we face the reality of our living hope of being raised eternally from the dead!

It is also a great day of receiving a great inheritance from our father in heaven

*Praise be to the God and Father of our Lord Jesus Christ! In his great mercy he has given us new birth into a living hope through the resurrection of Jesus Christ from the dead, and into an inheritance that can never perish, spoil or fade. This inheritance is kept in heaven for you, 1 Peter 1:3-4*

It is a day of graduation from the physical and the mortal to the immortal and also the beginning of our wait for a new heavenly body at the resurrection!

*For we know that if the earthly tent we live in is destroyed, we have a building from God, an eternal house in heaven, not built by human hands. 2 Corinthians 5:1*

Transition is the end of the race that is set before us

*I have fought the good fight, I have finished the race, I have kept the faith. Now there is in store for me the crown of righteousness, which the Lord, the righteous Judge, will award to me on that day —and not only to me, but also to all who have longed for his appearing. 2 Timothy 4:7-8*

So my final thoughts on the greatness of death are these

*'The day you enroll into school is great but not greater than the day of your graduation!'*

*'Returning triumphant from the battlefield is always better than the marching into war'*

*'The end of a great voyage is always better than its beginning, more significant in every way!'*

# 3

# Transition, its purpose

Transition has a purpose. It is not just transition or a point of death or termination of the life we know.

### *We live or die to the Lord*

I would like to begin with the concept of the great apostle Paul who was completely sold out to God. His philosophy in life was therefore that 'both our life or our death serves God's purposes'

*'For none of us lives for ourselves alone, and none of us dies for ourselves alone. If we live, we live for the Lord; and if we die, we die for the Lord. So, whether we live or die, we belong to the Lord. Romans 14:7-8*

What this means is that life is not a selfish affair. Even though you can walk through life being completely self centered we are all interconnected. What we do impacts the next person, and the next person, and the next, and the next in some way or the other. Paul is telling us that there is a higher purpose in life than just the proverbial 'me, myself and I'.

This is just the normal wisdom of the earth that we should all appreciate. Because many people have achieved great things just by 'not living for themselves'. The examples are many,

Mother Theresa, committed her life to care for the poor, sick, orphaned and dying. This simple vision led to a charity called 'Missionaries of Charity' in Calcutta, India which later spread to more than 130 countries worldwide. The impact on evangelism and sharing the faith of the son of God Jesus Christ was immense!

Nelson Mandela fought apartheid in South Africa and fought racial segregation. He served as South Africa's first black president and gracefully left office after his term as president.

Abraham Lincoln fought for racial equality in the USA and his efforts led to the abolishment of slavery and ultimately to his own assassination dying at the tender age of 56.

Lastly, Dr. Martin Luther King Jr. fought racial segregation. As an activist and humanitarian, he became leader of the African-American Civil Rights Movement and delivered his iconic 'I have a dream' speech followed by his assignation five years after his great speech.

What are we saying, not that you will be assassinated! but that those who have the most impact in life do not live for themselves and at times the price is quite high.

Secondly, we need to move from a selfless affair to a godly affair! When we move from simply being selfless to being godly we move from the mortal into the immortal realm of things.

Paul declares that 'if we live we live for God'. That's why he calls this life 'a race'. And says I have run the race. And fought the good fight

*I have fought the good fight, I have finished the race, I have kept the faith. Now there is in store for me the crown of righteousness, which the Lord, the righteous Judge, will award to me on that day —and not only to me, but also to all who have longed for his appearing. 2 Timothy 4:7-8*

I love another terminology he uses. He calls himself 'a drink offering!' That is being poured out for others and also to God!

*For I am already being poured out like a drink offering, and the time for my departure is near. 2 Timothy 4:6*

What a concept to live by! Can you imagine what it would be like to simply live your life not for yourself but for and to God! To consider yourself a servant of all and an actual sacrifice for the good and well being of others?

This mindset is really what was embraced by those whom we call great leaders of our day. If you study all those we have mentioned, none was self seeking. In fact they behaved so sacrificially that some of them became an actual sacrifice. They gave their lives or lost their lives and were willing to soldier on as they pursued their purpose in life in spite of the very real dangers that lurked in the shadows.

So, transition can be the price we ultimately pay for living for God. Because God expects that we not only live for him but we also die for him. Transition can be a direct price of serving God or it can be a mere acceptance of God's will at the conclusion of our days. Whatever it is, we need to come to the conclusion that even if we die, we die for the Lord.

But what if you don't have the opportunity to play some grand role in life? What if you're just a regular person just like the majority of us? Well, this is still a philosophy to live by. It is not only for the rich and famous, or for the anointed and 'called of God' alone... it is something which everybody should hold dear.

When you really think about it, it's actually a very simple and straightforward concept. It really means you simply want to honor God in all that you do! Even without fame or status, anointing or calling, the fact that we are honoring God in all we do is a calling in itself. It's the purpose of all creation to honor God just as it has been said that,

*'Let everything that has breath praise the LORD.*

*Praise the LORD. Psalms 150:6*

*'So, .....whatever you do, do all to the glory of God.*

*1 Corinthians 10:31*

So these scriptures teach us some interesting things. Firstly, we have a duty to honor God. Now if we replace the word duty with the word calling it means you have a calling to honor God! So don't say you are not called because you are! *You are called to honor God!*

If we replace the word duty with yet another word 'anointed' it means we have an anointing for the sole reason and purpose Of honoring God!

In fact John mentions this anointing when he says

*'As for you, the anointing you received from him remains in you, and you do not need anyone to teach you. But as his anointing teaches you about all things and as that anointing is real, not counterfeit—just as it has taught you, remain in him.*

*1 John 2:27*

We are anointed because we are in Christ the anointed one. And our anointing, calling and separation is simply to honor God!

*'But how can you achieve this?'* You might ask, 'how can we live to honor God with our lives?' I believe the answer is in putting God first in all that we do.

We should put him first in our decisions, in our giving, In our worship and making time for God in prayer and meditation of his word. It's simply a principle of God first! If God is first, everything you do will really honor God! And in whatever we do, we will really 'honor God'.

The scripture confirms this when it says

*'in all your ways submit to him, and he will make your paths straight. Proverbs 3:6*

I like the word 'submit' and it's also interpreted as 'acknowledge'. To submit is to yield. This means we should yield our will to God's will!

When you yield to God you will relinquish your own plans for his.

To yield is to stop resisting God. Some of us resist God in certain areas, it is time to start yielding to and to stop resisting his words, his command to repent, his command to obey and his command to follow him completely! So... stop resisting!

It also means to stop fighting! Some people attack and wrestle with God as a business or way of life and as part of their job description. Stop fighting God, or talking ill of his servants and his people who may naturally be weak and imperfect. Let's stop fighting God or fighting man!

To acknowledge is similar in meaning and means to 'consider the reality' of something. Perhaps it's time we consider God as real in all the decisions we make!

When we do so, we know our decisions always have consequences and will become more considerate of our actions.

It also means to accept a fact or a person that was previously denied. Perhaps there are some decisions you consider as not belonging to or requiring God's intervention? It is possible! It's time we start accepting God's interest in our little affairs of life. This is similar to one meaning of yielding which means to 'consent reluctantly'. It's an interesting word but perhaps it's high time we agree even though it's against our 'better judgement'. It's time to agree with God even though we would want to be in total control of ourselves. So even if it be reluctantly, please consent to God's involvement in your life.

It also means to accept as valid! This means to accept as 'an authority' or 'as important'. It simply confirms the importance of God in the decisions you're making and the actions you're taking. Remember.... God is important in all you do!

Lastly, to acknowledge also means to accept the true or intended role of someone. This means to accept that God is really Lord, Master and King of our lives and he should indeed influence our decisions because we acknowledge his Lordship and kingship over us! That is tough right?

This means complete surrender to him in everything. It really means yielding and surrendering to God.

When we do this we truly live for God!

*to honor him,*
*to love him,*
*to follow him,*
*to surrender to him,*
*to acknowledge him*
*to yield to him*
*to serve him; and*
*and simply to obey him!*

If we live in this manner, our death and transition will follow in like fashion! It will be for his glory! It will ultimately serve his purposes of coming to be in the father's house.

*After everything is said and done,*
*after all the dust settles,*
*after all the questions are asked,*
*after the confusion fades away*
*you will be in your father's house!*

### *We live ready*

Living ready is all about being prepared for death. It is an important mindset as it brings a strong perspective to life. It's about knowing you will die one day. It's about preparing for that day.

How do you know someone is living ready? We live ready when we have a will, that says how our estate should be managed. This avoids a lot of confusion in the event of death and helps protect your children and dependents from financial suffering. Don't die without a will! You will do a great injustice to your spouse or your children and dependents.

Living ready is not living in fear! It's about knowing you will die but knowing that there is life afterwards! There is a permanent home for us, far more glorious! Far more beautiful and far more alive and peaceful!

When people are gripped by fear, they do certain things for fear of certain death. They may stop riding a car, because they fear they will have an accident, they will stop driving because they had an accident in which a loved one died. I recall a friend of mine bought the book 'Supernatural Homecomings' for a friend of hers who had an accident in which her own daughter died. And she was driving! This can lead to a lot of guilt and fear. We may never do certain things again like driving. But we have to overcome our fears and not be paralyzed by death. I had to do the same and overcome my fear of driving. I had an accident in which I lost my dear wife so that I could not easily drive for quite a while, actually for 9 months! I think it's a normal fear to have but in time we simply need to overcome it. I often had minor panic attacks and some not so minor, that I would feel like parking the car until my heart stops racing. And I have parked it a few times just calm down.

I had to make a decision whether to continue being involved in branch church ministry that involved driving a long distance of about 1 hour each way for fear of increasing the risk of further accidents. But I had to overcome my fears and place my life in God's hands. I remembered that he who keeps his life loses it and he who loses his life finds and keeps it (Math 10:39).

Living ready does not mean despondency or a defeatist attitude. If you have a defeatist attitude you will not invest in anything meaningful because you think you are dying anyway! You will not pursue education, work well in a job. Plan for your own retirement or plan to buy land or build and buy a house, you will not pursue a business, or send your children to the best schools your resources can reasonably afford! No you will not do all that and you will simply resign to the fact that you are dying anyway and will be paralyzed by fear!

This can be a sad state of deception because the loss of meaning for life will make your life seem completely worthless and useless. You will let go of everything you once held dear, you will not fight for your marriage, not be engaged in your education or in your job, you will have actually died before your death. God does not want you to die mentally. When you do so, everything around you dies with you. The fire and energy is drained from you and nothing works because 'as a man thinketh so is he'. This is a death that is even sadder than physical death.

Once we give up mentally and spiritually even our bodies give up, our immune system is compromised and in fact we can physically die before our time! So live ready by planning 20 or 30 years ahead but live like you could go at any moment within your long term plans.

When you live ready you are able to say

*'For to me, to live is Christ and to die is gain. Philippians 1:21*

## *Death is certain*

The old adage says the only things that are certain in life are 'death and taxes'. Death is certain for several reasons. Firstly, it's because of the simple frailty of human life. We cannot live forever and try as we may, to keep young and fit and beautiful, we will certainly die. This is the way of all the earth.

Death is certain because it is necessary for our lives to bear fruit. When you consider a seed, it cannot germinate unless it is buried in the ground and dies (1 Cor 15:36). In fact what you sow is not what will germinate. You will sow a simple seed, but the shape of what germinates has little resemblance to the seed because it will have roots, a trunk, branches, leaves and fruit. It will be much more complex than the little and tiny, almost round, seed.

Death is certain also because our days are already numbered by God.

*"You saw me before I was born. Every day of my life was recorded in your book. Every moment was laid out before a single day had passed." Psalms 139:16 NLT*

*"You have decided the length of our lives. You know how many months we will live, and we are not given a minute longer."*

*Job 14:5 NLT*

The fact that we cannot cross the line or extend the line without God's permission is so clear! King Hezekiah could only live 15 more years with God's permission. He had to pray to God otherwise the prophet brought word from God that Hezekiah would die indeed.

And Job also confirms the fact that in fact it is God who sustains us and if he so wishes we would all perish. In fact without him we are nothing!

*"If God were to take back his spirit and withdraw his breath, all life would cease, and humanity would turn again to dust." Job 34:14-15 NLT*

If God has numbered our days, we have a graduation date! We have a homecoming date! We have an appointment with our master and father, and with Jesus the Righteous Judge!

# 4

# Transition, it's God's prerogative!

Prerogative is an exclusive right. It is a right or privilege reserved only for those to whom it belongs. It cannot be conferred or transferred to another. That's what transition is! Transition is God's prerogative!

We cannot claim it, we cannot demand it, we cannot question it even if we don't like it. It is not in our power neither is it our choice to exercise, it is totally and completely God's.

Jesus, when he was speaking to his disciples told them that times and seasons are not their concern. They are God's business. In fact Jesus almost seems to be shocked that the disciples wanted to know when he would establish his kingdom. May be he was shocked because in reality the question was so premature. It's now just over 2000 years since that question was asked. Yes two millennia! And Jesus is yet to establish his kingdom! Jesus was simply saying

*'hey dude! Mind your own business. Your business is to preach and mine is to establish God's Kingdom. My schedule is more than 2,000 years away so just do your thing and stay in your lane!'*

That's the same way he perceives our questions about, and our desire to control death! It's none of our business! We should just do what we've been told to do, fear him, love him, obey him and respect and acknowledge him in all we do! That's all! The rest is God's business. He has numbered our days, he has given us an hour glass filled with the sands of time! How many they are is not for us to count, it's for God alone to know!

Because it's His prerogative let's leave the time of our death in God's own hands!

### *Transition is unavoidable*

*"Indeed, how can people avoid what they don't know is to happen? None of us can hold back our spirit from departing. None of us has the power to prevent the day of our death. There is no escaping that obligation, that dark battle. And in the face of death, wickedness will certainly not rescue the wicked." Ecclesiastes 8:7-8 NLT*

The logic of this scripture is quite amazing. It firstly establishes or presumes that we do not know the time of our death neither the manner of our death. I think this point was not even belabored because it is a rhetorical question that needs no answer.

Secondly, it establishes the logical fact that you cannot avoid what you don't know! You can't have a contingency plan for it, and when it comes you just deal with it the best way you know how!

Then, it also establishes the fact that that the process of death is a process involving powers that are beyond us and beyond our strength and capabilities to the extent that in our weakness and lack of stamina to the power of God, we cannot prevent our spirits or hold them back when they are departing and leaving our body! It's again another logical fact based on the assessment of relative strength between God and man! It is therefore undeniable!

Lastly, a logical conclusion is made that because of all these three factors, none of us can ever prevent the day of our death!

In bringing home this fact it even says the power of the wicked will not help anyone! This is a divine revelation especially for those who think they have power, be it political, social, financial or spiritual, in order to prevent their death.

*"Riches will do you no good on the day you face death, Proverbs 11:4 GNB*

*"When Judgment Day comes, all the wealth of the world won't help you one bit. So you'd better be rich in righteousness, for that's the only thing that can save you in death." Proverbs 11:4 TPT*

Some people are deep into sin and deliberate service and worship of the devil. People like these can be satanist, spiritists, witches and wizards and those involved in the occult who literally wield the spirits of death, wreaking havoc and causing death and chaos in the lives of others.

Because they wield these powers, they are largely exempt from being attacked themselves because they are advancing the purposes of their dark lord Satan. But God says that even these people cannot escape death.

*"You boast, "We have struck a bargain to cheat death and have made a deal to dodge the grave. The coming destruction can never touch us, for we have built a strong refuge made of lies and deception." Therefore, this is what the Sovereign Lord says:*

*I will cancel the bargain you made to cheat death, and I will overturn your deal to dodge the grave. When the terrible enemy sweeps through, you will be trampled into the ground. Again and again that flood will come, morning after morning, day and night, until you are carried away." This message will bring terror to your people." Isaiah 28:15-16, 18-19 NLT*

God's power is so strong that all those who think they have made a covenant with death or have power to cheat death and to dodge the grave through meticulous planning will be destroyed. He promises to intervene on his own, to exercise his prerogative and to cancel all such deals with death.

In this passage I deliberately did not include the whole of verse 16. This verse talks of a remedy to the impending destruction.

*"Therefore, this is what the Sovereign Lord says: "Look! I am placing a foundation stone in Jerusalem, a firm and tested stone. It is a precious cornerstone*

*that is safe to build on. Whoever believes need never be shaken." Isaiah 28:15-16, 18-19 NLT*

When you read this verse it simply prophesies of Jesus who is the chief cornerstone and foundation stone. The message is clear,

*'instead of serving, sin, riches, pleasures or dark powers, you better serve Jesus. And ... when facing death you better be standing on a firm foundation! The foundation of Jesus Christ!*

*Transition is mysterious*

The prerogative of God is shown in his mysteriousness regarding how he does things. Indeed his ways are much higher than our ways and are definitely past finding out. And indeed when death is about to happen it is usually concealed. Shortly after the passing of my dad, my aunt and I were talking of how shocking and tragic it had been for all of us. We both said we didn't know that our taking him to hospital would lead to his death. We all thought he would walk out of hospital and not die. Perhaps if we knew what would happen we would have avoided his death somehow? But the Bible says how can one avoid what he does not know is going to happen? The solace we find was that we all wanted him to get better, the doctors did their best, he fought to the very end but at the end of it all, God took him home.

But why does God conceal death? I think there are practical reasons and spiritual reasons. Perhaps it would be even more sad if people knew their time of death. For some this is seen when doctors become forthright regarding a person's medical condition, perhaps some would be so devastated and depressed that they would literally die before their time! Oh yes! This is seen in both how, and how many people quickly deteriorate and die once told they have a terminal illness like cancer and HIV/Aids for example. Some things are just too difficult for us to handle and are better left to God. About secret things, Moses said secret things belong to God! (Deuteronomy 29:29).

The wisest man to have ever lived said in fact God takes pride in his 'concealment' of things. As God, of course he wants to remain with some level of mystery. We can't fully understand God. Indeed *"It is the glory of God to conceal a matter."* Proverbs 25:2 KJV

In the fourth chapter of 2Kings, Prophet Elisha who frequently received a word from God once told a barren Shunemite woman that she will be of child by a certain time the following year. This prophecy came to pass and the woman bore a child. But he was later surprised to hear of that same child's death when he had grown up a little. When this woman mourned her son she fell at Elisha's feet wailing in deep distress, the prophets aide, Gehazi, wanted to push her away but Elisha stopped him from doing this and made a stark confession which I can only render as

*'Leave her alone because she is broken in heart, and I actually share in her pain and I am even more surprised that God has concealed this from even me! So I also am at a loss for words'*

Elisha was at a loss for words because he usually got a word from God about what God was going to do or what would happen. He was a prophet after all! But even he, experienced the mysteriousness of death. 2 Kings 4:27.

## *The mysterious will of God*

The will of God is, to begin with, 'the will of God!' This uncanny description tells it all! It is sometimes pleasing to us as men but sometimes it's totally unpalatable. This too is a mystery.

Shall I talk of David who prayed for the life of his son? David prayed and fasted for the son he bore with Bathsheba to be spared from death. He used the theology he knew and learned from the relationship he had always had with his God. He knew God as a merciful God, as a God who answers prayer, a God who loves him and a God who can save the life of his son. Though he heard God's verdict over the child, his confidence in the word and nature of God led him to believe that the child will live.

But lo and behold! The will of God was that the child would die.

Similarly, the Lord Jesus when faced with death asked for it to pass him by. He asked in deep anguish with tears as drops of blood, but at the end of it all he had to yield to the will of God!

Another story I like is the story of Jesus' disciples who wished for the establishment of a Jewish kingdom to liberate them from Roman rule. When asked about this in Acts 1:7 he simply said it is not for you to know the times and seasons that are set by my Father's own authority!

As we have said before, Jesus was telling them,

*'first of all you should mind you own business. You don't have the right to know when God wants to do something. Only God has that power, that privilege and that prerogative. I know you want a kingdom but you have no authority to know when it will come!'*

I think this principle is so true to us all! It is something that I learnt after the passing of my wife Debbie, her passing was so sudden and so unexpected as all car accidents are. I had a million questions in my head until I really understood what Jesus was telling his disciples here. I learned that it's not for me to know God's timings. I learned that the times set by God are set because, and as a result of, and through God's own authority! And more so, I learned that this authority is not shared with anyone. It's 'his own' 'his very own!' God does not share his glory with man. And even on the mysteriousness of death he is not going to share his glory with anyone! So he keeps it a mystery because he does not want to cause more pain, he is God and that is his glory and his own authority and lastly, it is according to his own will!

So how does God make death mysterious? Through concealing it and shrouding it, and making sure that no one can actually see it.

## *God has the power over life and death*

I am again reminded of the story of the rich fool, God called him a fool because while he was planning about how to spend his bounty of crop he gave no thought to the fact that his life is in God's hands and, in fact, God said 'this very night I am taking your life'. This tells us that it's God's prerogative. That's why Hannah, in her prayer, also says it is God who gives and takes life, it is his prerogative indeed!

### *God's power over death*

*"The Lord brings death and makes alive; he brings down to the grave and raises up."* 1 Samuel 2:6 NIV

There are various renderings to this verse in different versions which are 'to bring', 'to cause to occur' and 'to have the power to do so.'

Other renderings say 'he kills', meaning that he can do so deliberately in judgement as he did many times in the Bible.

He promised to kill the rulers of Moab in Amos 2:3

The sons of Aaron, thought they could bend the rules of holy sacrifice by offering strange offerings and unholy prayer and were burned by God's angry fire! Lev 10:1-3.

In the time of Noah he killed roughly 20 million people through drowning because they were wicked (Gen 2:7)

He judged and burned the cities of Sodom and Gomorrah for being very wicked and attempting to rape two Angels. Could they even have managed to do so? I wonder! They were burned to death by fire and a rain of burning sulfur (Gen: 19:4-5. Ezek 46-50).

God killed the first born sons of Egypt by sending the Angel of Death because pharaoh resisted God and denied the Israelites from worshiping their God (Exo 12:9).

He killed the Egyptian army when they tried to follow the Israelites into the Red Sea (Exo 14:28).

King Ahazia was killed by God for being faithless and seeking medical advice and help form a rival god to Yahweh! (1 Kings 22:51, 2 Kings 1:16).

God hates faithlessness and grumbling so that the ten faithless spies were killed with a plague because they spread doubt and disbelief when God had promised them the land of Canaan (Numbers 14:36:38).

102 soldiers were burned to death for being impolite to Elijah and serving King Ahab. (2 Kings 1:9).

God sent 2 bears to maul 42 youths simply for laughing at Elijah's bald head! (2 Kings 2:23-24).

For simply not worshipping God, some foreigners were killed by lions in 2 King's 17:25-26.

In 2 Kings 19:35 as 185,000 soldiers slept, an angel of the Lord slew them all in their sleep. Their only crime was 'fighting God's people!'

The ground opened up and swallowed Korah and friends for claiming they were as holy as Moses and considering themselves his equal. (Numbers 16:27-32).

God struck Nabal dead for ill treating David and also struck the Philistines with death and tumors for capturing the ark of God.

*"So they called together all the rulers of the Philistines and said, "Send the ark of the god of Israel away; let it go back to its own place, or it will kill us and our people." For death had filled the city with panic; God's hand was very heavy on it."*

*1 Samuel 5:11 NIV*

Even in the New Testament God killed a few people but evidently they were less perhaps because it was the age of grace.

We all know the story of the deceptive couple Ananias and Sapphira who thought they could get the glory of giving, supposedly, all they had to God while withholding some to themselves and even attempting to deceive not only the church, and the apostle Paul, but even the Holy Spirit (Acts 5:1-10).

And lastly King Herod who thought he could share the glory of God, neither stopped people from calling him a god nor glorified the true God and was therefore both struck by an angel and then eaten by worms! (Acts 12:23).

Friends, God can kill! He just chooses not to do so but it's up to us to learn why God kills and to avoid similar sin.

### *God's power over life*

But God does not just kill he also gives life and there are similar examples of this as well. While bringing death may be considered a divine prerogative of God. Bringing life is simply an amazing miracle! It shows that he is the source of life and he has the ability to give life to whomever he wills, even after death!

A certain widow in Zarephath was commanded to take care of

prophet Elijah. After a Miracle in which her flour and oil was multiplied, the widow's son fell ill and died. Distraught and in sorrow the widow brought her son to the prophet accusing him of reminding God of her sins and bringing God's judgement in her home. Elijah prayed to God asking for life to return to him and the Bible says God heard Elijah's cry and life returned to the boy! 1 Kings 17:17-24.

The son of a Shunemite woman had a sharp headache one day and fell dead. His mother took him and put him in an upper room she had prepared specifically for Elisha a prophet of Jehovah who usually lodged with them. This child was an only child and had only come about because the prophet blessed her with a miracle from God. She was barren you see, and only managed to conceive when God promised her a child through the prophet. It was this only son that had died. She quickly sent word to the prophet. When the prophet came he performed a miracle and warmed the boy's body. The boy sneezed seven times and came back to life (2 Kings 4:18-37).

One fellow with very unusual luck was, first of all, quite unlucky to have died. His death occurred after prophet Elisha had died and was buried. The fellow in question was being buried close to Elisha's tomb when the grave diggers saw a band of Moabite raiders approach. Fearing for their lives they simply threw the body of the unlucky fellow into Elisha's grave. As soon as the body landed on the bones of Elisha, divine resurrection power flowed through his body and zapped him like a bolt of divine electricity, instantly bringing life to his cold and stiff lifeless body! The fellow instantly stood on his feet, and walked out of the tomb and immediately headed home! (2 kings 13: 20-21).

King Hezekiah's story is one of my favorites. The man was told his days are over and he needed to put his house in order. However he cried out to God and God heard his prayer. After the prophet told him to prepare for his death God literally sent him back to the king. The narrative gives the impression that immediately the prophet prayed, Hezekiah had the audacity to ask for a second chance at life. Before the prophet left the palace the king managed to touch God's heart. The master of the universe changed his mind and told the prophet Isaiah to go back and tell him that God will give him life! Isaiah turned around just before the middle court of the place and delivered the new message!And indeed he lived 15 more years! That is the power of prayer! (2 Kings 20:1-6).

A very moving story is told of Jesus who met a funeral procession in the city of Nain. It was a funeral of an only son and to make things worse, it was the only son of, not just any woman, but one who was also a widow. The heart of Jesus literally went out to the woman as he could see her face covered in tears and her clothing drenched in the same. The sorrow on her face was too painful not just for her but even for Jesus to bear. He came to her and embraced her holding her up in the crushing weight of her sorrow. Comforting her he said 'Don't Cry'. All other mourners told her to be strong, accept God's will and hope for the best but Jesus said, 'don't cry', in his mind, I'm almost sure, he continued and said '*I am the author of life, I am the resurrection and the life and I will help you!*' So he quickly left the woman and went to the coffin. He made no promises he simply said 'young man I say to you get up!' And remarkably the young man got up.

In fact when you know who Jesus is you can only but conclude that he was saying '*I, the author of life, the resurrection and the life, the great I am, say to you get up!*' And obeying the order, the young man sat up and began to talk (Luke 7:11-17).

Jesus also had an encounter with Jairus, a synagogue leader. He came to Jesus asking that he heal his sick daughter. As Jesus journeyed to Jairus' home a message came that his daughter had now died. But Jesus told him not to worry and to just believe. When he arrived at Jairus' house he entered the room where the little girl's body lay and taking her hand he said 'My child get up'. I find that very interesting he did not only say 'little child get up' but actually 'My child'. I think he was operating from the perspective of a creator of the universe and claimed ownership of this child. Yes she was Jairus's daughter but in actual fact she was Jesus' daughter by virtue of being his creation! And indeed Jesus protects his little children! (Luke 8:52-56).

In John 11 we read the story of Lararus who was a friend of Jesus, as were his sisters, Mary and Martha. Lazarus fell ill and word was sent to their dear master Jesus about this illness. But Lazarus died before Jesus could heal him.

Jesus arrived about 4 days later, and Mary and Martha bemoaned his delay, saying Lazarus would not have died if he were early.

Jesus tried to explain who he really was and the power he had and that he was in fact the author of life. First he told his disciples, before setting off for Bethany, that *'Lazarus is asleep but I will wake him up'*. Since they were not understanding him he plainly said that 'Lazarus is actually dead but I will raise him up'.

He tried to say the same to Martha in what was a rather frustrating conversation

*'your brother will rise again'*

*'Yes at the last day he will rise'*

*'Hey Martha I am the resurrection and the life! Today you already have resurrection power'*

In frustration with this doctrinal debate Jesus asked *'where have you buried him'*

On the way to the tomb, Mary came and immediately fell at the feet of Jesus in sorrow together with all the mourners who wailed with her. A holy anger brewed in the heart of Jesus. Remembering that in the beginning man did not need to die but now faces the pain of death because of Adam's sin in the Garden of Eden. Touched by empathy himself, he too wept. It was emotionally challenging even for Jesus even though he had a mission to raise Lazarus he saw the pain all around him and mourned with them in empathy and deep care. Anger welled up inside him at this phenomenon called death! It was not God's design for man to die and see corruption. To rot in the grave and be forgotten. Man is the very image of God and death is not reflective of an eternally living God! Not at all. He was angry at the loss, at the pain and confusion and sense of helplessness that death caused and his heart was pumping hard! More than eager to raise Lazarus up! He was angry that Lazarus had died a young man, way before his time. Jesus' emotion was an emotional concoction of not only sorrow but also a high dose of anger! You couldn't pick out which emotion dominated. But it was clear that in the melting pot of emotion, deep in his heart, anger was not in short supply!

Arriving at the grave, blood pumping through his veins, shaking with emotion, a surge of resurrection power built up within him and he demanded the tombstone to be rolled away. The Spirit of God stirred up within him! The well spring of life welled up within him and mixed and entwined itself in the words of Jesus!

*'Lazarus come out'* he shouted and the dead man heard the voice of Messiah, the anointed one, the creator of the earth and all creation! The dead ears made up the words and comprehended what they meant. The dead man did not hear these words from the tomb.... No no no, he was in Sheol by this time. It was already 4 days since his death and he was now in the place of the dead. But the words of Jesus boomed in Sheol! Like the sound of many waters. Lazarus could not believe it! He was being given a second chance in the land of the living. In a moment, his spirit was let loose from his apportioned abode in Sheol.

The gates of Sheol opened for him. The angels carried him from there and in an instant he was levitated from the depths of the earth to his tomb. But his body was lifeless, and had already started seeing corruption. It was four days since he had died and his body was already decomposing, but miraculously power flowed in his body like a zap of electricity flowing from the crown of his head to the soles of his feet.

All the decomposition started reversing. All the fluids oozing out of his body dried up. It was as if a new body was being created right there in the tomb. A new sense of life and freshness was simply consuming the old one. It was as if the darkness of corruption was running away from the light of life that was shining through each and every cell of his body. The blood that had solidified in every vein and capillary of his body, liquified again, every bacteria that flourished within him died in an instant and the contagion and poisoning in his blood disappeared as it was consumed by the freshness of the creative power of Jesus, Messiah and the author of life! It was inexplicable and indescribable, Lazarus was an observer of the very creative power of God, His spirit was in his body but was also outside of it as he saw the master at work within him.

He was a witness of creation, the recreation, restoration, cleansing, purification and revitalization of his body! What a marvel to watch! He had a privilege that only the Holy Spirit had as he watched and participated in the world being created by God. He, Lazarus, shared in this privilege of witnessing creation too!

*"I was there when he established the heavens, when he drew the horizon on the oceans. I was there when he set the clouds above, when he established springs deep in the earth. I was there when he set the limits of the seas, so they would not spread beyond their boundaries. And when he marked off the earth's foundations, I was the architect at his side. I was his constant delight, rejoicing always in his presence. And how happy I was with the world he created; how I rejoiced with the human family!" Proverbs 8:27-31 NLT*

This is what Job was told and asked by God,

*"Brace yourself like a man, because I have some questions for you, and you must answer them. "Where were you when I laid the foundations of the earth? Tell me, if you know so much. Who determined its dimensions and stretched out the surveying line? What supports its foundations, and who laid its cornerstone as the morning stars sang together and all the angels shouted for joy?" Job 38:3-7 NLT*

Lazarus surely did not witness the whole creation but certainly had a glimpse of it as his spirit saw the resurrection power of God work on his body! All this happened at the command of Jesus! At the command of three words and by the time the words of Jesus had reached into the tomb his spirit was summoned, by the time Jesus words echoed out of the tomb his body was restored, renewed and recreated! Lazarus' soul came into and reunited with his body and in an instant was able to feel his body! He could move his limbs, he could hear his heart pumping liquified blood! He could feel the blood surging through his body and could move his legs again. Though wrapped in burial clothes he had to come out of the tomb into the land of the living! And lo and behold Lazarus walked out of the tomb to the astonishment of Mary, Martha and all the mourners! Jesus had shown himself to be strong and mighty! And the author of life. (John 11).

The next resurrection that occurred after this was that of Jesus himself. No resurrection has ever been and will ever be more significant than that of Jesus. For without this resurrection all resurrections are meaningless! This is the focal point of scripture. While in all resurrections the people died again, it was not so with Jesus. He resurrected to live forever! To be the first fruit and firstborn from the dead

*"But now [as things really are] Christ has in fact been raised from the dead, [and He became] the first fruits [that is, the first to be resurrected with an incorruptible, immortal body, foreshadowing the resurrection] of those who have fallen asleep [in death]." 1 Corinthians 15:20 AMP*

*"And He is the head of the body, the church, who is the beginning, the firstborn from the dead, that in all things He may have the preeminence." Colossians 1:18 NKJV*

*"He is also the head [the life-source and leader] of the body, the church; and He is the beginning, the firstborn from the dead, so that He Himself will occupy the first place [He will stand supreme and be preeminent] in everything."Colossians 1:18 AMP*

Jesus' resurrection was announced by an angel just as his birth was. Mary went to the tomb to anoint Jesus' body But an angel met them and said he is risen!

*"But the angel said to the women, "Do not be afraid; for I know that you are looking for Jesus who has been crucified. He is not here, for He has risen, just as He said [He would]. Come! See the place where He was lying." Matthew 28:5-6 AMP*

In fact, they were even asked *'why do you seek the living among the dead!'*

The death and resurrection of Jesus made us to be forgiven and justified before God, and ensures our eternal life because he said

*"since I live, you also will live."John 14:19 NLT*

Jesus did not resurrect alone. As the author of all life and of life that truly overflows, he also resurrected the bodies of righteous people. The Bible records that on his resurrection the earth shook and many tombs were opened. In addition to this, the resurrected bodies of the righteous were seen walking in Jerusalem at the resurrection of Jesus. What a proof they were of Jesus as the resurrection and the life! Because these people appeared to many within the city, Math 27:50-53.

After Jesus' resurrection there were two more resurrections that occurred. There was that of Dorcas and Eutychus.

Dorcas's story is a heartwarming one, she was literally saved by her good works! When she died everyone remembered how helpful and kind she was to the poor and needy and also to the believers. She always made clothes for the widows and so the believers could not accept her death. They deliberately kept her body in a special room and instead of proceeding with a funeral service they decided to call for Apostle Peter. As if praying to God, the believers pleaded their case with Peter because they knew that Peter was a contact point with the miraculous power of God! In them the scripture about believing God's prophets in order to prosper was strong in their minds (2 Chron 20:20). Peter had no choice but to come and pray for this woman. He silently prayed to God just like Hezekiah did. Reminding God of all the good works done by Dorcas in her life, just as Hezekiah did, and afterwards he felt a strong conviction in his heart that God is about to do something, to honor the faith of not just one but many saints. The seed of faith was strong, they were all in one accord, he could already feel the presence of the Spirit of God saturating the room and it felt like the windows of heaven's miraculous and glorious blessings had already opened ! All he needed to do now was to remain in tune with heaven and the life giving Spirit of Jesus! And with deep conviction, and in a bellowing voice, he gave a command to her lifeless body saying 'Dorcas rise up!'

Dorcas' body was lifeless, cold and stiff, and perhaps stayed so for a day or more since Peter was called from a different city. And also, factoring in the deliberations of the believers on what to do and the time of travel to the next city to seek the apostle Peter. It could be narrowed down to comfortably being two or more days. But, this stiff and lifeless body heard the command of Apostle Peter and Dorcas' spirit returned to it. She opened her eyes and sat up! Peter helped her to her feet and presented her alive to the believers!

Lastly, there is an odd story of a young man called Eutychus! This young fellow could not endure the long sermon of Paul. Sitting on a window he drowsed himself to sleep and fell from the window that was three stories high and fell head first to the ground!

Apostle Paul stopped his sermon and rushed outside to the pavement where he fell. The scene was ghastly, with a cut in his head, blood flowing from the young man's ears, and mouth! Surrounded in terror by the whole congregation of believers. As Paul walked closer to the body of Eutychus, the crowd gave way as he walked straight through. He stood over his body, knelt down and prayed for him while putting his arms around him.

The crowd witnessed a creative miracle as the crack in his skull closed up accompanied by a snapping sound, of bones coming back together, then the skin that was hanging wide open closed back together with no sign of a scar! As I imagine it.

Instantly he came back to life and was brought up into the upper room where they had a meal together with the Apostle and everyone was relieved and encouraged! I guess the moral of the story is 'never sleep in a sermon!'

*Other evidence of God's life giving power*

In addition to all these marvelous deeds of giving and taking life we see the miracles of healings that litter the Bible. Healings of people with chronic illnesses like the woman with the issue of blood. Healings of people at the point of death like the centurion's servant and miracles of people who were simply born lame or were plagued with an ailment. Healing of other illnesses in many people such as Simon's mother who was stricken by acute fever.

What I know is that any serious illness has the potential to cut short someone's life. This means that the healings of people who were not necessarily at the point of death were indeed potential deliverances from death. So, both living in a state of divine health and the divine act of actual healing is a gift God uses to ensure we are not only healthy but that we also fulfill our time and days on this earth.

So I pray that may 'God bless you with the blessing of healing and the blessing of divine health!' Divine healing is not only the curing from disease but also the state of remaining healed and also not falling ill and of being protected from illness! May this divine healing guard the full number of your days on earth and make sure that not one of them is robbed from you and not a second is lost!

The conclusion of all this discussion is that God can bring death but also God can raise up. He can bring death as in bringing it at an appropriate time. When he brings it at the appropriate time what remains is for us to prepare for our journey because it is his will. In this case he makes all things work together for the good of those who love him. It is an unpleasant experience but unfortunately it is the way of all the earth until such a time that death is destroyed completely at the end of days.

When God brings death he provides us the strength and comfort to face the rest of our days and to be hopeful of the inheritance of the eternal life we have in God! When he brings death he also takes care of those that remain behind on this earth.

God can also execute judgement and bring death as he judges. He can raise up from the dead after losing your life or can raise you up when you are near the grave by destroying and preventing whatever attack the enemy brings!

All in all. He has power over death. Because Jesus conquered death and has the keys of life and death!

### *God has power over timing and types of death*

As we all know, people die in different ways. Some in their sleep, some due to sickness, some accidents, some being attacked and so on and so forth. There is even a program dedicated to the science of death on television called '1,000 ways to die'. All bearing testimony that the methods of dying are many.

Unfortunately even this is something we have no real power over.

Our days are both numbered and laid out before God so that he knows what is to happen before each of them came to be!

*"You saw me before I was born. Every day of my life was recorded in your book. Every moment was laid out before a single day had passed." Psalms 139:16 NLT*

Now if God numbers our days and he knows them before each of us are born. Then in his book He should be able to know how we will actually die. In fact the scripture above indicates that he knows each of our days. And I believe this applies even to the day of death. Before it comes to pass he has known it already and fully.

Jesus, for example knew that he would die on the cross and would be pierced. Jesus and God knew this because it had already been prophesied by the prophets of old who declared that he would be a 'man of sorrows pierced for our transgressions' ( Isaiah 53, Zechariah 12:10). He also knew that none of his bones would be broken and indeed this came to pass in john 19:36'

He also knew about the death of Siserah over whom it was prophesied that he will be given in the hand of a woman and indeed it was a woman who killed him with a tent peg as he slept in a tent. Judges 4:9,21

Lastly Jesus knew what the type of death of James and John would be like. The mother of these two disciples wanted a great honor for them in heaven. She wanted that they sit in the second highest seats, one on his right and one on his left. Essentially this was a hard thing because perhaps that's God's prerogative. However, Jesus hinted to her that it's not only a hard thing, but there is also a high price to pay for that. The price was a cup of suffering. Such honor does not come cheaply. Just as Jesus was described as the suffering servant anyone who shares in his glory in heaven would equally share in a similar path and experience. As a result, he simply asked if they could partake in the cup of suffering from which he himself would drink! And the mother, intoxicated by the prospects of heavenly glory, ... said yes!

History records that James was thrown off from the pinnacle of a temple, and then beaten to death with a club! John however died of extreme old age.

I thought of highlighting this as a matter which may help others gain closure as to why we have lost our loved ones in the manner that we have. As indicated elsewhere in this book, I lost my father to illness in the course of writing this book it was a battle that spanned about 3 months and even though we were hopeful, God called him home. Barely a week after he passed a close friend of mine also lost his father. His father simply collapsed due to a cardiac arrest. I was shocked when he told me about it because it was so sudden. At the funeral a lot of thoughts crossed my mind. I wondered who between us would have easier closure. People say if someone is ill for a time you are more likely to get closure because at least you saw them ill as opposed to sudden death from an accident or such as the one my friend's dad had. While it may seem true I think death is difficult in all circumstances. I still struggle to understand why we lost the fight with my dad's illness, I replay the sequence of events time and time again to try to understand what else could have been done better, this continuous analysis could be as traumatic as wondering why my friend's dad, simply collapsed, wondering what could have been done to prevent it and what signs were missed if there were any! And, according to the family, there weren't any signs to indicate he could succumb to a heart attack.

Another sudden loss for me, as already mentioned, was the death of my wife whom I lost in a car accident in which we were both involved in. I find myself in a similar situation as my friend who suddenly lost his dad. I ask similar questions as what should I have been done to avoid this drunk driver who came into our lane and rammed into us. Should we not have driven that day? I equally have a million questions that are equally asked by many others, my friend included.

So what do we do when faced with such circumstances? I think we simply have to accept that it has happened but also accept that it is God who knows how and when we will be called home!

As I stood beside my friend, Tapu, at his Dad's funeral, a thought came into my mind. I thanked God that he had lived 9 years more than my Dad. And I actually wished my Dad had lived those 9 more years. I also wondered if my prayers for nine more years and prayers for my dad to be healed would have eased my pain of losing him. The answer was no! Unless he had lived to be extremely old, perhaps the pain would have been less. But even then the pain of loss remains deep, as it was when I lost my 105 year old grandma some few years earlier.

So, I concluded that perhaps the timing of death is not the true remedy to our pain. Because our pain is all about the fondness and depth of love for those we have lost and this does not always depend on the time someone has lived. It is simply an umbilical cord that is severed at the point of death. And regardless of its time, it hurts! And it hurts deeply. Even my sister's death 4 years back hurts when I go through all the questions I want answered. Even though she died of illness as well. It's not really different coz every loss hurts in its own way!

So if the timing and nature of death are things we have no control of, what should we do? and how do we deal with the trauma and questions that arise with it? I think the best way is to say 'it's God's prerogative' he knows best and if we leave it into his hands our minds are more at rest and we stop contending with a million questions. And if we do, we remind ourselves that it's God's prerogative until our mind is put to rest.

So my final thought on this is,

*'Make peace with God's timing …The later death is deferred the later the pain is equally deferred. It does not make it any easier that someone was given more time. What matters is the assignment and purpose being lived and fulfilled on earth.*

# 5

# Transition, how it happens

Transition is a spiritual process and how it happens largely depends on who it is happening to. There is the transition of the righteous and of the wicked and we shall see it mostly from the perspective of the righteous. *This is a deeper discussion of our introduction of what death is with some additional information and examples so don't see it as pure repetition.*

### *An open door and visions of heaven*

In my book, Supernatural homecomings' I write real life accounts of people who transitioned miraculously. There was a common thread across these stories that amused me and that I never knew was backed by scripture. One thing I heard across the stories was the statement 'my door is open' or 'my way is open' and indeed 'heaven is open'.

Now there is one instance that comes to mind in which the heavens were opened and it was when Jacob used a rock for a pillow and he saw a stairway getting into heaven! He had a vision of heavens gates with the angels of God ascending and descending on it.

*"As he slept, he dreamed of a stairway that reached from the earth up to*

*heaven. And he saw the angels of God going up and down the stairway."* Genesis 28:12 NLT

My own sister, before she passed, asked my mom

*'Do you see the curtain Mum? There is a white shiny curtain over there? They are calling me to go, they are calling me to go behind the curtain…'*

another instance of heavens opening is when Jesus ascended into heaven. The disciples had a glimpse of heaven but could not see it fully.

*"After saying this, he was taken up into a cloud while they were watching, and they could no longer see him. As they strained to see him rising into heaven, two white-robed men suddenly stood among them. "Men of Galilee," they said, "why are you standing here staring into heaven? Jesus has been taken from you into heaven, but someday he will return from heaven in the same way you saw him go!""* Acts 1:9-11 NLT

*"As they strained to see him rising into heaven, two white-robed men suddenly stood among them. "Men of Galilee," they said, "why are you standing here staring into heaven? Jesus has been taken from you into heaven, but someday he will return from heaven in the same way you saw him go!"" Acts 1:10-11 NLT*

Later on in the Bible we read of Stephen who was being stoned to death. Now for him the heavens were really opened, because as he was being stoned, he saw through the gates of heaven and saw the Glory of God,

*"And he told them, "Look, I see the heavens opened and the Son of Man standing in the place of honor at God's right hand!""*

*Acts 7:56 NLT*

So one thing I know is that there is a door that opens for us into the heavens, into the gates of heaven and that the heavens themselves welcome us as they remain hidden no longer.

## *Visions of Jesus and his Glory*

One thing that happened to Stephen is that Steven saw Jesus standing at the right hand of God. Now, please note that Jesus is standing not seated. Jesus is so in tune with Steven that he can feel Stephen's pain and anguish! He couldn't sit down. But what he does here is that he strengthens and encourages Stephen. The power of seeing Jesus is that we are encouraged and he shows us the glory and reward that awaits us in heaven! Apostle Paul speaks of this and says,

*"Yet what we suffer now is nothing compared to the glory he will reveal to us later." Romans 8:18 NLT*

So even though Stephen was being painfully stoned, he was encouraged by Jesus and by the glory that so far outweighed the pain and suffering he felt as he was being stoned!

So the encouragement we have is that the process of death itself is a suffering that is literally 'nothing' when compared to God's promised glory in heaven! In fact it's not even worth comparing to the glory and reward of heaven. I recall the story of apostle Peter, he also died by crucifixion but he asked that he be crucified upside down! Why?...Because he did not think himself worthy or qualified enough to die in the very same way that Jesus his Lord and Saviour had died. To him the pain of an upside crucifixion was nothing when compared with the prize of being reunited with his Lord and Saviour!

This somehow comforts me, it encourages me that no matter how we die, we cannot compare death with the glory that comes through this painful experience. Some people die peacefully while others die after a long battle with illness and others in so much pain, others die instantly on the occurrence of an event, perhaps a car accident, perhaps cardiac arrest, or other event that takes them suddenly. I think despite how we transition what matters is that we have a reward in heaven where we are going to!

So, Stephen not only saw the glory of heaven but more importantly Jesus himself! And there is yet another mystery about seeing Jesus!

*"Beloved, we are God's children right now; however, it is not yet apparent what we will become. But we do know that when it is finally made visible, we will be just like him, for we will see him as he truly is." 1 John 3:2 TPT*

*"But friends, that's exactly who we are: children of God. And that's only the beginning. Who knows how we'll end up! What we know is that when Christ*

*is openly revealed, we'll see him—and in seeing him, become like him." 1 John 3:2-3 MSG*

There are two important things we see here, we see the vision of Jesus and the vision of his glory!

So Paul is effectively saying,

*I can't really be sure how to explain how good it will be! How good our spiritual bodies will be! What I know is that there is a trigger to our transition and translation. First we shall see Jesus! Then we shall see his glory! And you know what? once we see him, we will yearn to be with him! Once we see his glory, this glory envelopes and surrounds us so much that we are transformed into the image of the Jesus that we see!*

This scripture mainly applies to the second coming of Jesus, but what we see from Stephen's story is that Jesus also appears to us as we transition. We also see that the glory of God that is revealed to Christians on the rapture is also seen here in some measure, when Steven is losing his life to persecution!

It's is also repeated when Paul talks of what happens when we behold God's Glory!

*"But we all, with open face beholding as in a glass the glory of the Lord, are changed into the same image from glory to glory, even as by the Spirit of the Lord." 2 Corinthians 3:18 KJV*

*"All of us, then, reflect the glory of the Lord with uncovered faces; and that same glory, coming from the Lord, who is the Spirit, transforms us into his likeness in an ever greater degree of glory." 2 Corinthians 3:18 GNB*

There is something totally amazing about this scripture! It says when we behold Jesus with our unveiled and uncovered face 'we literally become what we see!' Also what we see is 'as in a glass', this entails looking through something. Just like seeing into the spiritual from the physical and we see a vision of Jesus the perfect one! Perhaps this is what happened to my sister as she 'looked through the curtain'.

Therefore, when we see this Jesus something remarkable happens!

Firstly, glory radiates and is transferred and reflected onto us! This is the glory of Jesus! It reflects on us and hits the surface of our spiritual body. The Bible says we behold 'the Glory of the Lord' that is 'coming from the Lord' and as a result of this something else divine follows!

We are changed into the very same image! In other words we are transformed and changed into the image and likeness of Jesus!

That's why Paul's says '*when we see him! We will become like him!*'

Friends, the point of transition is the point at which we become like Jesus! Perfect and completely sanctified by the sin washing blood! Never to fall sick again, never to die again and never to suffer again! Friends the transition of a christian is a marvelous mystery! And a marvelous process.

I recall a conversation I had with my good friend and brother Zenzo as he consoled me on the transition of my father. I lamented at how he battled with his illness until his last breath and how it was very painful for me and the family to see him fight during those last moments. Zenzo gave me a testimony of what happened to his pastor friend who had suffered a heart attack. He was quickly airlifted to hospital by a helicopter ambulance. Whilst in flight the paramedics did all their best to safe his life. Finally they saw that they were losing him. But the wife could not allow him to go. The situation was traumatic for them but she pressed the paramedics to do all they can to save him. And as they continued they finally got a pulse back and he slowly started to breath again and until his life was saved. His wife was so happy and thanked God for saving his life.

As the husband got better and eventually got out of hospital he was not at all pleased to be alive! Much to her surprise and dismay of course! The husband told a very different story to what the wife experienced. As he drifted into the other life he said he felt God's overwhelming peace! He said he was not suffering as they saw him suffer on their way to the hospital, he was completely covered by the presence of God, and while they panicked he had a glimpse of God's glory. He was taken into heaven but was soon being sent back. He pleaded to stay but he was told his work was not yet finished and that his family still needed him. He argued with God, that she can't be destitute because God is able to care for her and the family, he gave all sorts of reasons why it was ok for him to stay in heaven but God said 'no' that's when he heard his wife shouting at the paramedics to do all they can. He resuscitated and got a pulse back! Much to his disappointment. Zenzo told me it took him four full months to forgive his wife for resuscitating him.. four full months! Friends,... the glory of God is amazing it is like a cloud that engulfs you and ushers you into the presence of Jesus! When you have a glimpse of this glory. His peace overwhelms you and you are attracted and pulled like metal to a magnet into heaven! This gentleman did not want to come back to earth after what he saw, he just saw marvelous and beautiful things.

According to 2 Corinthians 3:8 all this happens By the Holy Spirit. Now who is the Holy Spirit? He is the spirit of Jesus! It means we are not alone! Even in death! Jesus is the Good shepherd and in death he shepherds us and leads us, and his Spirit translates us into the heavens!

## *Hearing the shepherd's voice*

As mentioned elsewhere in this book, the point of death is the point of hearing the voice of our shepherd.

*"My sheep listen to my voice; I know them, and they follow me."*

*John 10:27 NLT*

This takes me to my sister's story who said 'I am being called beyond the curtain! When we hear his voice we obey and follow him! A friend of mine Dharles had a clear revelation of this. Once she heard of my sister's passing all she said was *'she has heard the voice of her master'*.

I was curious about this response until I remembered that indeed the sheep of Jesus listen to his voice.

## *walking into the light*

Jesus describes himself as the light of the world! And so I am persuaded to believe that when we die the light of Jesus shines on us. Though our body shuts down and our eyes grow dim, we are not left alone in darkness. We have Jesus who is the light of the world!

*"Jesus ... said , "I am the light of the world. If you follow me, you won't have to walk in darkness, because you will have the light that leads to life."" John 8:12 NLT*

I can again make reference to my sister's passing and to her experiencing bright light and this was not at the point of death this was about 2 days before she died. That is why I am persuaded that as we pass on to heaven the light of Jesus shines upon us. Just as it shone on Stephen when he was being stoned. So do not fear the darkness because the darkness of death can not overcome the light of Jesus that shines within you!

*"The light shines in the darkness, and the darkness can never extinguish it." John 1:5 NLT.*

On the contrary those who deny God have been known to experience darkness and blackness even before their body actually dies.

### *Putting off the tent*

As discussed earlier, this body is a temporary dwelling place, it's just a tent! It's a shack and not a mansion! It's something to help us as pilgrims and visitors on this planet earth! Just like an astronaut needs a space suit to survive in space, our bodies are 'earth suits' that help us live and survive on earth. Well a time comes to go home and when this time comes, we put aside the tent to wear clothing that is more permanent. We are given a spiritual body in heaven! and this temporary earthly clothing is put aside.

*"For we know that when this earthly tent we live in is taken down (that is, when we die and leave this earthly body), we will have a house in heaven, an eternal body made for us by God himself and not by human hands." 2 Corinthians 5:1 NLT*

The book of Job also talks of the fact that we have simply been clothed with this body, with bones, flesh and muscle and therefore we are not to be identified with our clothes. We are not our clothes, we are in fact more than our clothes.

*"Thou hast clothed me with skin and flesh, And knit me together with bones and sinews." Job 10:11 ASV*

Somehow the tone of this verse is as if Job's spirit was already there when his body was being made as if he was observing the workings of God this points to the fact that even before we were born, we existed in the eyes of God!

### *Carried by angels*

I have heard intriguing stories of my relatives being welcomed by angels as they transitioned. I later found out that the stories I heard are actually backed up by scripture! The story of Lazarus and the rich man reveal this fact. It paints a stark contrast between someone who is going to heaven and someone going to hell. Read this passage carefully...

*"Now it happened that the poor man died and his spirit was carried away by the angels to Abraham's bosom (paradise); and the rich man also died and was buried."* Luke 16:22 AMP

*"Then Lazarus died and God's angels carried him away. They put him at the side of Abraham in heaven. The rich man then also died and his family buried him in the ground." Luke 16:22 EASY*

This passage says Lazarus's spirit was carried by the Angels of God into heaven! Wow, this means believers are never alone! However, the rich man was not taken to heaven. On the contrary his spirit went to a place called Hades where the spirits of the unredeemed and unsaved dead go to await judgement.

The contrast we see is that Lazarus went heavenward while the rich man went downward and was simply 'buried'. And the Easy translation of the Bible emphasizes how much of a human affair it was. It was perhaps a nice funeral but it says *'his family buried him'*. That's a sad thing for anyone. If we are simply buried without knowing Jesus as your Lord and Saviour, you cannot go to heaven! You can have an elegant funeral but as long as you don't have Jesus, who is the light of the world, you cannot be carried by God's angels.

I pray that you will be carried by God's angels! I pray that if you have not received Jesus as Lord and Saviour you receive him and commit your life to him today!

A terrible story I heard from a close friend of mine is a story of his cousin. The cousin was a lady who could not move and could not walk due to her illness. On the day of her death, she saw terrible beings come and take her into a deep darkness, deep down into the earth. She shouted for help and refused that those demons should take her and as she struggled she got off the bed and held on to it. She struggled like this for a while and by the time she died, she had twisted and bent the metal hospital bed so that the bed had an oval shape. She was in such torment that her spirit is the one that energized her weak body as she struggled to hang on to her life and her bed. But once the moment of transition comes, there is nothing you can do. You have to go!

So choose to follow the voice of Jesus and be carried by his angels rather than being taken by angels of death and Satan's demons into hell!

## *Safely in God's hands!*

The point of transition for a believer is where our spirits are safely in God's hands! When we lose loved ones we want to know they are not 'lost' and that they are in a good place. We want to be sure that we ourselves are going to be safe when we die. Well, the Bible has something to say about that!

First of all Jesus says that no one is able to steal his sheep from God's hand and this knowledge gives me great assurance.

*"The sheep that are My own hear My voice and listen to Me; I know them, and they follow Me. And I give them eternal life, and they will never, ever [by any means] perish; and no one will ever snatch them out of My hand. My Father, who has given them to Me, is greater and mightier than all; and no one is able to snatch them out of the Father's hand." John 10:27-29 AMP*

Jesus promises to give us eternal life and he also says as emphatically as possible that *'they will never ever perish'* and also that *'no one can snatch them from My hand!'*

Wow! I don't know about you but that gives me great relief right there! You know what, I thought getting into heaven is almost an impossible task!

Considering how human and flawed I am! What if I sin unwillingly, what if I think wrong thoughts, what if I fail God in some way? All these are questions that arise in my mind. But I am reminded that salvation is not really by works, it is by grace and believing that the blood of Jesus was shed for my sin. Not just my sin before I received Jesus, but even my sin when I have already received Jesus as my Lord and Savior! The blood of Jesus is enough for you. And this blood speaks of better things than the blood of Abel! This blood cries for mercy and grace, for forgiveness and pardon!

Jesus knew how safe he was in God's hands and therefore put his spirit in God's hands through prayer and Stephen did the exact same thing!

*"Jesus called out with a loud voice, "Father, into your hands I commit my spirit." When he had said this, he breathed his last."*

Luke 23:46 NIV

*"While they were stoning him, Stephen prayed, "Lord Jesus, receive my spirit."" Acts 7:59 NIV*

So, a believer's spirit is safe and secure in the hands of God!

## *Prepared by God*

God has his own way of preparing people for transition. A friend of my late wife Debbie, shared with me one of my wife's meditations and preachings she shared on their prayer group shortly before she passed,

*"At day's end I'm ready for sound sleep, For you, GOD, have put my life back together." Psalm 4:7-8 MSG*

*"In peace [and with a tranquil heart] I will both lie down and sleep, For You alone, O LORD, make me dwell in safety and confident trust." Psalms 4:8 AMP*

She was preaching on the confidence we have of laying our lives in God's hands and of sleeping in peace. This was prophetic to me because it was God's own way of saying she was at the end of her earthly day on this earth and she was ready to lie down in the sleep of death.

Also it shows how prophetically she foretold of the peace that fills our hearts when our time comes. The psalmist says we lie down and sleep in peace and with a tranquil heart. The reason we have peace is that God protects our spirits and we have confident trust in God!

On a different occasion and within a month of her passing she also shared on Isaiah 61:1-3 which talks of beauty for ashes.

*"The Spirit of the Lord Jehovah is upon me; because Jehovah hath anointed me to preach good tidings unto the meek; he hath sent me to bind up the broken-hearted, to proclaim liberty to the captives, and the opening of the prison to them that are bound; to proclaim the year of Jehovah's favor, and the day of vengeance of our God; to comfort all that mourn; to appoint unto them that mourn in Zion, to give unto them a garland for ashes, the oil of joy for mourning, the garment of praise for the spirit of heaviness; that they may be called trees of righteousness, the planting of Jehovah, that he may be glorified." Isaiah 61:1-3 ASV*

She said that ashes only come after a devastating fire and that in life challenges and fires will come, and of such degree as to burn up life as we know it and that God's children are not exempt from life's troubles. But our hope remains in the fact that God wants to take that pain upon himself!

She specifically talked of people who grieve and mourn due to various degrees of loss. Whose fires of life have consumed them so much that just from looking at the ashes you can't tell what has been burnt or destroyed. But it's in that situation in which God turns up. He is ready to heal and restore and pour on you the oil of joy instead of mourning. So, no matter what you're going through, God will restore your joy if you run to him and praise him through your storm!

She shared these messages within 2 to 3 weeks of her passing. Her friends remembered this message when they heard of her passing and were convinced that somehow God was preparing her!

Finally, in the week she died, she shared a prophetic scripture of her social media profile that we all agreed to use for her memorial and it prophetically talked of the glory that awaits us in heaven!

*"The future glory of this Temple will be greater than its past glory, says the Lord of Heaven's Armies. And in this place I will bring peace. I, the Lord of Heaven's Armies, have spoken!""*

*Haggai 2:9 NLT*

*"The glory of this latter house shall be greater than of the former, saith the Lord of hosts: and in this place will I give peace, saith the Lord of hosts." Haggai 2:9 KJV*

This verse, by far, is what all her friends and family were talking about. Something peculiar was happening to her in her last days, she was just on fire for God in a different way, her friend described her as literally and completely sold out to God and ready to do anything for her Lord!

To us this verse spoke of her transition to a glorious place where her body, which is the temple of the Lord, will be replaced with a more glorious body in heaven!

All in all there was one thing that struck me the day she died. She was so quiet and calm. All through the day, she wasn't talking much she was just so quiet. Her spirit was resting in God!

## *Something foretold*

Sometimes God goes to the extent of foretelling your transition. I believe that most of the times this is personal to the person transitioning and they normally don't tell others about it. The testimonies I have heard about transition show that God ministers to the person who is transitioning either openly or discreetly and in a way that is sometimes unclear. As far as an open revelation is concerned, I think it depends on the level of intimacy we have with God.

*"And the Lord said, Shall I hide from Abraham that thing which I do;"* Genesis 18:17 KJV

This scripture shows us that the Lord has been caught up in the ropes of care and affection before. He debated whether he should hide his plan to destroy Sodom from his friend Abraham. The story of Abraham's friendship with God shows us that friendship and companionship with God helps us get the grace to receive this foreknowledge.

Elijah's transition was equally *foretold, and we see that the sons of the prophets told Elisha that 'don't you know that your master will be taken away from you?'* He was asked this question twice, and he confirmed on all occasions that indeed he was aware of this. And later Elijah himself revealed it and offered him one last request before he was taken.

*"Then the group of prophets from Jericho came to Elisha and asked him, "Did you know that the Lord is going to take your master away from you today?" "Of course I know," Elisha answered. "But be quiet about it."" 2 Kings 2:3, 5 NLT*

Jesus also knew that he would die a sacrificial and painful death and he often spoke of his death to his disciples. On the day of his death he asked for the disciples to stand with him in prayer and he himself prayed to God with tears.

Paul also experienced this. I believe this is what happened to Paul when he said that his time of departure is near and he said this on several occasions including when he said *"As for me, my life has already been poured out as an offering to God. The time of my death is near." 2 Timothy 4:6 NLT*

As for Apostle Peter he disclosed that the Lord Jesus had clearly revealed to him that his death was near. He surely was not given the exact date, all he knew was that it would be soon!

He also described his body in ways similar to what we have seen before as something that must be 'discarded'

*'since I know that the putting off of my body will be soon, as our Lord Jesus Christ made clear to me.' 2 Peter 1:14*

So, in all this we see that God is able to foretell your transition.

### *Translation*

Translation is defined as 'the act of changing in form, shape or appearance'. I believe this is what happens in the spirit and this fits well with Haggai 2:9, which talks of a more glorious temple and also 2 Corinthians 5:8 and 9 which says we look to a heavenly house and that, in fact, we yearn for it.

*"For in this we groan, earnestly desiring to be clothed upon with our house which is from heaven:" 2 Corinthians 5:2 KJV*

This scripture emphasizes the fact that at the point of death we are translated from the physical to the spiritual. And that we wear a new and eternal body. My friend Mizeck recounted his experience when he was taken towards hell after suffocating on his bed. He recounts of how much more sensitive his spiritual body was! He recounted that he could literally sense every cell in his body, he instantly knew everything that surrounded his body the moment he died, even the location of a cup and of a teaspoon were imprinted on his mind in the most accurate of details as his spirit left his body. And he was not even going to heaven at that time, what more if our spiritual bodies are glorified with the glory of Jesus as was the case with Stephen!

In the Bible I believe there are 3 people who experienced a complete and 100% translation. Most of us will loose our bodies to the grave until the resurrection. We will have spiritual bodies in heaven as we await the resurrection of our physical bodies. But for these three gentlemen all of them experience a complete 100% translation with no physical body to be raised on resurrection day. I think these are the only 3 physically gloried bodies in heaven! As far as I know of course!

I will deliberately start with the second gentleman because he gives us a very vivid picture of how the translation really happens. He is Elijah!

Scripture records that Elijah was taken by a whirlwind into heaven. But, what this means I really don't know.

*"As they were walking along and talking, suddenly a chariot of fire appeared, drawn by horses of fire. It drove between the two men, separating them, and Elijah was carried by a whirlwind into heaven." 2 Kings 2:11 NLT*

Elijah's translation had both a chariot of fire and a whirlwind. I believe that the chariot came with a guard of angels just as all believers are carried by angels into heaven, the chariot was befitting that he may ride in glory, in honor and like a victorious prince of heaven who was a mighty servant of God!

The whirlwind was a glorious wind of the spirit. That covered the chariot on which he rode into heaven (Others have understood this passage to mean that Elijah did not ride the chariot but actually rode the whirlwind. So as a non theological student, I will only focus on the spiritual significance of the whole event and not necessarily the mechanics of it).

I am reminded of Acts 2 which talks of the day of Pentecost. The Bible says the Holy Spirit fell on the disciples with a sound of a mighty and rushing wind and with tongues of fire sitting on their heads. As said before, I am no accredited bible scholar but with my lay man's eyes I see elements of the Spirit of God appearing on Elijah's translation that also appeared on the day of Pentecost. I see wind, and the noise that comes with it, and I see fire.

Elijah had a chariot and horses of fire, while Pentecost has tongues of fire, 120 of them one for each disciple, this was a lot of fire, don't be fooled by the description of them as tongues, combine them together and it was a huge fire!

I also see the sound of a mighty rushing wind, which the NLT describes as a 'mighty windstorm' the noise and power of such a wind is also seen in the noise and power of a whirlwind.

So what is the conclusion? There was the glory and Spirit of God at work in both occasions.

That's why Paul says our translation into the image of Christ as we behold his face is 'by the spirit of the Lord'!

*"But we all, with open face beholding as in a glass the glory of the Lord, are changed into the same image from glory to glory,* ***even as by the Spirit of the Lord.****"* 2 Corinthians 3:18 KJV

*"On the day of Pentecost all the believers were meeting together in one place. Suddenly, there was a sound from heaven like the roaring of a mighty windstorm, and it filled the house where they were sitting. Then, what looked like flames or tongues of fire appeared and settled on each of them. And every-*

*one present was filled with the Holy Spirit and began speaking in other languages, as the Holy Spirit gave them this ability."*Acts 2:1-4 NLT

So this is what I believe happened to Elijah, *'mortality was swallowed up by immortality'*

His mortal body was swallowed up and consumed by the immortal body which welled up from the fuel and power of the Holy Spirit deep within him! I think there was so much power and fire of the Holy Spirit that literally flared up his immortal body to swallow up his physical body, so that the spiritual body now overtook, consumed as a flaming fire, and became, his new body! I am reminded of Moses and the burning bush whose leaves did not get destroyed to ashes even though it burned. In the same way there was a combustion and a changing of his physical elements at the cellular level that literally changed the physical into the spiritual. But not just a spiritual body, no a real physical body with so much glory and capability that it can survive hyper speeds that are faster than the speed of light passing the planets into heaven. He was literally given a resurrection body! The body that all believers will get when Christ Jesus comes at the rapture. At the rapture Jesus will revive, upgrade and recreate, bodies that have faced decomposition, but with Elijah he translated a living body, with all the organs working inside him. Elijah was Reengineered in his body by the Holy Spirit of the living and Almighty God! That whirlwind and that fire of the Holy Spirit reflected the Glory of Jesus Christ on his mortal body and as a result, *mortality was instantly swallowed up by immortality!*

Now let's go to the first person to be translated and he was none other than Enoch! His translation was perhaps the most enviable. It is not one by a prophet like Elijah but by someone like you and me who simply enjoyed God's fellowship! The Bible simply says and Enoch walked with God and was not 'For God took him'.

I like Enoch's story because it is a story of companionship with God and how that companionship can bring you into God's presence. From what is written in the Bible I deduce that the fellowship with God was so strong that Enoch did not live as long as his fathers such as Adam and others who mostly lived for an average of close to 1,000 years.

Enoch's fellowship with God was so sweet that God had to call him home early. Enoch died at 365 years, just over a 3rd of the average lifespan of the day! I find that amazing. Lesson in point? .... Sweet fellowship with God can call you to deeper fellowship in heaven. God so loved Enoch that he wanted him walking in heaven with him!

Enoch was also carried into heaven perhaps not by angels but by God himself! Wow! Maybe there was no whirlwind but he simply received the direct first hand reflection of the glory of God in his body, and beholding the face of the Lord God almighty, he was transformed into the glorious image of God by the Holy Spirit. In sweet fellowship and companion he could well have entered heaven, hand in hand with his God, not carried by angels at all. Oh how sweet this fellowship can be. Perhaps it can be as a friend of God like Abraham, perhaps merely as child inheriting the kingdom of his father in heaven. Perhaps as a good and faithful servant, but whatever the relationship it was sweet and and it called him home!

So, Both Elijah and Enoch never saw death! Wow, what a privilege it is to simply walk into heaven! With your body not having to die! That is simply amazing.

For these two gentlemen we can really just speculate what type of bodies they got. Perhaps it's the final version of the body that is similar to the one to be given to the saints on resurrection day, perhaps it's a heavenly body, that will again be upgraded as the bodies of other believers are raised and upgraded. Whatever it is, is not as important as the fact that they have been translated into a higher form of glory than that of then earthly body. And for the other questions, that is something for God to worry about and not you and I.

The last person to be translated was Jesus Christ! On resurrection day the angels of God came and opened the tomb of Jesus Christ by rolling the stone. Whatever happened to Jesus we know that the body he received was no child's play, it was both physical but completely supernatural. Thomas Didymus was told to touch the body of Jesus and put his finger in his nail scarred hands! We know that Jesus ate fish with his new body! So it was a truly physical body. However it was a resurrection body! A divine and fully upgraded model with supernatural capabilities. We read that Jesus could travel long distances and simply appear and reappear. We read that the body of Jesus was not restricted by physical matter and that he could walk through walls! Literally walk through walls! If that's not amazing I don't know what is!

So whatever happened to Jesus, it also transformed his earthly body! I am reminded of the mount of transfiguration whereby the glory of God left both Jesus' face and his clothes shining like the sun! Wow! This gives us a glimpse of the body we will get on the resurrection day. And this body was also taken up in heaven by a cloud of God's glory! Jesus was taken into heaven in broad daylight as the disciples watched!

This physical translation however is so rare that so far it has only happened 3 times in all of human history. But I believe it is God's way of reassuring us of the resurrection and of its certainty! Jesus is the resurrection, if you have Jesus you have life and life eternal! Life when you die and life when he comes back to earth on the rapture as he takes his saints home. Remember, this is an instant translation Paul says that in an instant we who are alive will be caught up, and changed and translated

*"**In a moment**, in the **twinkling of an eye**, at the last trump: for the trumpet shall sound, and the dead shall be raised incorruptible, and **we shall be changed.**" 1 Corinthians 15:52 KJV*

This is what happened to Enoch, Elijah and Jesus! They were changed in the twinkling of an eye and the corruptible was swallowed up by the incorruptible.

*"For this corruptible must put on incorruption, and this mortal must put on immortality. So when this corruptible shall have put on incorruption, and this mortal shall have put on immortality, then shall be brought to pass the saying that is written, Death is swallowed up in victory. O death, where is thy sting? O grave, where is thy victory?" 1 Corinthians 15:53-55 KJV*

## 6

# Premature transition

Transition can sometimes occur prematurely. Medically, this means death before the average age of death for any population or nation. This differs from country to country but in general it means 'something that is too soon or uncommonly early'.

Premature death is, however, not simply defined as unpalatable death because death is naturally unpalatable. Unpalatable death can be one that is unexpected, sudden, death of the young, of those that are newly born, or unborn or even of newly weds for example. It can simply mean an undesired death. And this is characteristic of all death and normally it's regardless of the circumstance.

So what is premature death? Well, spiritually, I think it means something else. I personally believe it is when we die before the days that God himself has set for us, but more importantly it is when we die without achieving the purpose we were meant to achieve on this earth. An example is the potential infant death of Jesus. When he was still a baby, Herod wanted to kill him because Herod felt threatened by the prospect of another king who may potentially overthrow him, or so he thought (Mathew 2:16-18).

If Joseph and Mary would have exercised their rights to freedom and societal honor they might have chosen to abort Jesus. It would have been an unplanned pregnancy and an intrusion into their courtship, according to today's logic Jesus was an unwanted child. And if aborted, where would we be today?.

Pharaoh commanded that all male children under a certain age be killed! If Jesus had been killed at this time, he would not have become the Saviour of the world. If Jesus did not know the word of God when he was tempted by Satan to fall from the pinnacle of the temple he would have died a foolhardy death and not a sacrificial death on the cross. So, I believe that we are all on a mission to fulfill the purpose of God in our lives and this mission has a timeframe in which it must be achieved. If we die before achieving this purpose we have died prematurely!

Our purpose was foreordained according to scripture

*"For we are his workmanship, created in Christ Jesus unto good works, which God hath before ordained that we should walk in them." Ephesians 2:10 KJV*

And according to psalm 139 this purpose was allowed a timeframe.

*"You saw me before I was born. Every day of my life was recorded in your book. Every moment was laid out before a single day had passed." Psalms 139:16 NLT*

This means immediately we are born there is a countdown timer that is running and counting down every second that passes by, every breath you breathe and every heart beat you beat.

Because of this we ought to cry like the psalmist cried saying *"O my God, do not take me away in the midst of my days." Psalms 102:24 AMP.*

### *Why premature death comes to us*

Premature death comes for all sorts of reasons. One reason is lack of wisdom. Lack of wisdom comes in many forms, such as denying God and his word of instruction. It also means relying on your own strength and not on the guidance of God.

*"Hear, O my son, and receive my sayings; and the years of thy life shall be many." Proverbs 4:10 KJV.*

Sometimes we make decisions in life which are human and carnal and not led by God. Sometimes things are not always as they seem and they need spiritual discernment for us to know the right path to take. If we rely on our own strength we can easily err and choose a deadly path! May God give you the wisdom to choose the right path in life and not one that will result in premature death for you because

*"There is a way which seemeth right unto a man, but the end thereof are the ways of death." Proverbs 14:12 KJV*

Perhaps a case in point is Samson. Samson took for himself a beautiful Philistine prostitute obviously against the advice of his parents and even the will of God. He was a strange Nazarite. One who would not just serve God through sacrifice but one who would also rule God's people and deliver them from their enemies.

So his marriage to the prostitute was a marriage of deceit from the very beginning. It's like living with a pet constrictor in your home. A python is a python. It will play with you for as long as it cannot constrict and swallow you but once its big enough it will size you up, strangle you, and swallow you whole!

The challenge of Samson was 'to conceal the secret of his strength'. This was the point of contention throughout their marriage but instead of keeping his secret concealed deep in his heart he succumbed to the python of seduction. Delilah taunted Samson time and time again, seducing him through her feminine prowess and all her feminine endowments to finally constrict and crush the bones of Samson's will. As a python wraps itself around its victim squeezing tighter and tighter with each victim's breath, and each exhale providing an opportunity for a tighter grip, Samson ran out of options every time he found an opportunity to exhale! He initially gave away a reason that was not the true source of his strength. But this opportunity to breathe was one less reason to give because he could not use that reason again and slowly ran own of reasons until the truth was literally squeezed out of him! Delilah eventually found his secret and constricted and overpowered him

*"She tormented him with her nagging day after day until he was sick to death of it. Finally, Samson shared his secret with her. "My hair has never been cut," he confessed, "for I was dedicated to God as a Nazirite from birth. If my head were shaved, my strength would leave me, and I would become as weak as anyone else."" Judges 16:16-17 NLT*

The rest of Samson's story is well known, he was overpowered, eyes sadistically gouged out and made to work in a mill. Once his hair grew back he cried out to God that he would be given strength to destroy his enemies and the Bible records that he pushed down the pillars of the temple filled with philistines so that he killed more in his death that he had ever done in his life! Well it's both a good and sad ending. He killed more of his enemies than ever before, that's good, but he died early and had he lived longer with his eyesight he might have achieved more!

It's important that we remain and hold on to the wisdom from heaven and not rely on our own understanding whenever we are doing anything in life!' May God help us avoid what seems right in human eyes but eventually brings death to us!

*"Whoever abandons the right path will be severely disciplined; whoever hates correction will die." Proverbs 15:10 NLT*

The other reason is our living in sin. Jesus describes how the devil works and says he only comes to steal, kill and destroy but Jesus came that we should live fully and abundantly! John 10:10

*"Be careful that you do not die too soon. That might happen if you are a fool or a bad person." Ecclesiastes 7:17 EASY*

*"Do not be excessively or willfully wicked and do not be a fool. Why should you die before your time?" Ecclesiastes 7:17 AMP*

The Bible clearly points out that foolishness will cut short your days on this earth. He also gives a stern warning, don't be a bad person! Don't be too bad or excessively wicked, don't even be willfully and devotedly wicked he says if you do this ' you will die too soon'!

*Sins that invite premature death*

The Bible has several sins that are an abomination to God and will surely invite premature death.

Human sacrifice is abominable before God and he has promised to cut short our lives if we pursue it. This involves ritual abductions and killings of people such as albinos, wanton abortions of innocent children something that happens around the world and is condemned by God!

*""Moreover, you shall say to the children of Israel, ' Any Israelite or any stranger residing in Israel who gives any of his children to Molech (the god of the Ammonites) [as a human sacrifice] shall most certainly be put to death; the people of the land shall stone him with stones. I will also set My face against that man [opposing him, withdrawing My protection from him] and will cut him off from his people [excluding him from the atonement made for them], because he has given some of his children to Molech, so as to defile My sanctuary and profane My holy name." Leviticus 20:2-3 AMP*

Spiritism and consulting the dead such as is done by mediums and those that seek them is also a terrible sin before God.

*"'As for the person who turns to mediums [who consult the dead] or to spiritists, to play the prostitute after them, I shall set My face against that person and will cut him off from his people [excluding him from the atonement made for them]." Leviticus 20:6 AMP*

If you disrespect or curse your parents you cannot live long on this earth, in fact God promises a long life if we honor our parents!

*"'If anyone curses his father or mother, he shall most certainly be put to death; he has cursed his father or mother; his blood is on him [that is, he bears full responsibility for the consequences]." Leviticus 20:9 AMP*

*""Honor (respect, obey, care for) your father and your mother, so that your days may be prolonged in the land the LORD your God gives you." Exodus 20:12 AMP*

*"If you despise your father or mother, your life will flicker out like a lamp, extinguished into the deepest darkness." Proverbs 20:20 TPT*

There are Christians who would rather honor their pastors or spiritual fathers more than their own parents, that is a big mistake. Honor your parents above anyone else and you shall live long!

This issue of respect seemingly is not just limited to parents, it looks more like it applies to elders in general but more particularly if they are Holy servants of God, do you remember that God sent 2 bears to maul

42 youths simply for laughing at Elijah's bald head! Yes let's not forget that story! (2 Kings 2:23-24)

Adultery also makes the list of things that bring premature death. So don't do it. It brings illness and also a curse upon your life!

*"'The man who commits adultery with another's wife, even his neighbor's wife, the adulterer and the adulteress shall most certainly be put to death." Leviticus 20:10 AMP*

Incest is a common culprit for premature death! Don't do it, it's not godly and must be avoided. Incest is described as sexual relations with siblings or parents or parents in law! (Leviticus 20:11-12)

Homosexuality has always been a controversial subject but God, says it too will attract premature death, just ask the citizens of Sodom and Gomorrah! (Leviticus 20:11-12)

Bestiality is sexual relations with animals, sounds strange? Well it is strange! And don't do it. Shockingly there are people who do these things in this perverse world! (Leviticus 10: 15,16)

Have you seen anyone too smart for God? Who believes that they can trust in their own wisdom or strength? such people speak all sorts of nonsense against God and literally blaspheme his name! The verdict is the same '*death to the blasphemer!' Leviticus 20:16.*

Have you seen people who kill and murder as a way of life? Those who think they can play God on this earth and determine who lives and who dies! Murderers too inherit the curse of a premature death ! Leviticus 20:17

And my personal favorite, is those who are false prophets and peddle the Gospel of Jesus, taking the ministry as a business , they hype up the gospel and turn it into a fan fair. False teachers teach things that are indeed contradictory to God's word! They even teach things that defend their carnal and fleshly desires. They live a completely worldly lifestyle and they go to great lengths to defend themselves. Some even listen to demonic teachings and propagate them. God has a special promise for such. He says their destruction will be swift!

*"But there were also false prophets in Israel, just as there will be false teachers among you. They will cleverly teach destructive heresies and even deny the*

*Master who bought them. In this way, they will bring sudden destruction on themselves." 2 Peter 2:1*

*Overcoming premature death*

Death is a spiritual enemy and therefore it requires spiritual means to overcome it when it attacks prematurely. The most powerful weapon we can use in the moments we are being attacked by the danger of death is prayer. We need to fight back in prayer as much as possible.

*discernment*

The book of Job reveals certain secrets of how to wage this spiritual war.

To effectively pray, the first weapon God gives us is spiritual discernment. We have to be spiritually alert to interpret the spiritual environment and also to see and hear what God is saying. Sometimes God can be speaking to us in a subtle way. Perhaps with a deep sense of concern and at times through dreams and perhaps visions. The book of Job puts this very well

*"For God speaks again and again, though people do not recognize it. He speaks in dreams, in visions of the night, when deep sleep falls on people as they lie in their beds. He whispers in their ears and terrifies them with warnings." Job 33:14-16 NLT*

Some people have a gift of dreams which God uses to speak to them. They may think that it's just a nightmare while it's actually God giving them a warning of a spiritual attack. In such circumstances we ought to bend the knee and pray. Sometimes it's not very clear who the dream is all about but even so we need to pray and if you have the gift of praying in tongues you should pray in tongues as much as possible. This is because when we pray in tongues our spirit is praying mysteries that are directly inspired by the Holy Spirit. Such prayers are more direct, impactful and specific. Whenever you get that burden to pray please pray even if it's in the middle of the night.

This happened one Saturday morning. A friend of mine received the urge to pray and all she found herself praying about was preservation and protection and God led her to pray for me specifically. She prayed and prayed in the early hours of the morning and part of the day. She did not understand why she got this burden to pray. That very afternoon I had an accident in which my wife died. After a few weeks she came together with her husband to offer their condolences. She told me that she did not understand the purpose of her burden to pray until she heard that my wife and I had been involved in a car accident. She later heard that my wife died and that I survived. This is a difficult story to tell because it is not only personal but also sounds selfish. From a human perspective I don't understand why I survived the accident and my wife did not. You will therefore rarely hear me publicly thank God that 'I survived' because, humanly speaking, I would have chosen that my wife would have survived. When you think about home keeping and raising our two kids I am less capable to do a sterling job than my wife would. She just naturally had the motherly instinct inside of her to wake up early, prepare the kids for school, cook and raise them in a godly way. So, humanly speaking I don't understand why I survived. However, all I know is that there was this sister in the Lord who obeyed the voice of God to pray for preservation and when I heard her testimony I thanked the Lord that in his wisdom he at least kept one of us alive to provide for the kids. That for me is a more humanly understandable reason. So here I am thanking God that my kids are not both fatherless and motherless.

Anyway, the point of it all is that God speaks to his people to pray against premature death! And he wants us to be discerning in every way. Discernment comes through spiritual sensitivity and maturity. This can entail being sensitive to a person's lifestyle that perhaps may contradict with the principles of long living. Such as any of the sins we have discussed as causing a shortened life. If we repent or pray for grace and mercy, God can intervene to protect from premature death.

*Covering children with sacrifice*

This principle, of both prayer and sacrifice is also demonstrated by Job who used to offer sacrifices on behalf of his children. The reason he did this is that after his children held parties he feared that perhaps in their drunken stupor they had cursed God. However, even though he prayed, God had different plans that allowed the devil to take all

Job's children by death in a spiritual attack. We can see that Job was very spiritually discerning, he always covered his children with prayer so that if they sin God will always forgive their sin. Therefore if anything should happen to them and their lives are unexpectedly taken and are standing before the judgement seat of God, their sins are at least forgiven. This is something that every parent should do to their children. We should always pray for them to be washed and justified by the blood of Jesus Christ that was shed for all men!

The act of discernment involves observing actions, tendencies and lifestyles that can trigger premature death as discussed earlier. Once we see any thing like this we should immediately and constantly cover such people with prayer. We should pray for God's mercy and also pray that the Holy Spirit should turn their hearts toward God. Sometimes these can be your enemies but let's pray for them to be convicted by God and turn away from their wicked ways. Above all we should always pray that God will save them before they leave this earth!

*Standing in the gap*

What we see from the book of Job is that God uses various methods to protect from premature death. Apart from warnings and visions and dreams God uses the conviction of the Holy Spirit to turn away our hearts from the evil that cuts short our lives.

*"He makes them turn from doing wrong; he keeps them from pride." Job 33:17 NLT*

God helps overcome our pride and stubbornness so that we become humble. God is able to change people's hearts and when we pray we ought to stand in the gap for those who are bound by sin, praying that God will 'turn their hearts!' The Bible says this about God

*"He protects them from the grave, from crossing over the river of death." Job 33:18 NLT*

It also says

*"They lose their appetite for even the most delicious food. Their flesh wastes away, and their bones stick out. They are at death's door; the angels of death wait for them. "But if an angel from heaven appears— a special messenger to intercede for a person and declare that he is upright— he will be gracious and*

*say, 'Rescue him from the grave, for I have found a ransom for his life.' Then his body will become as healthy as a child's, firm and youthful again." Job 33:20-25 NLT*

This talks of people who are physically weak and are battling with sickness, those who are wasting away, and are at death's door, and even angels of death are ready to take them. God says if someone is found to play the role of an angel or a 'God send' or 'messenger of God' or simply put, 'an intercessor' God will save that persons life!'

I remember a chat I had with one of my pastors who collapsed and was close to death. She could see her body laying on the floor. Her workmates took her and put her in a car and sped to the hospital which was about 4 kilometers away. She says the team that took her were praying for and over her all the way to hospital. However she noticed that their prayers lacked fervency and commitment. They were more filled with fear than faith. Arriving at the hospital she still was unconscious but could still see her body as they tried to help her, in her spirit she knew that her colleagues were no longer praying and were now quiet, waiting for the doctors but she felt in her spirit that they needed to continue to pray their weak prayers even at that time, she tried to speak to them but because she was in the spirit they could not hear her. Slowly she saw the distance between her spirit and her body increase meaning that she was closer and closer to death. By God's grace, God intervened in the weak prayers of her colleagues and she came back to life. She told me that this experience taught her that whenever we stand in the gap our prayers should be sincere and they should not be filled with fear. Had it not been for the grace of God, she says, 'I would have died that day!' But God graciously intervened in spite of prayers that were not too fervent and indeed were partly filled with the fear of death itself.

So whenever you stand in the gap for someone firstly be be available, because *'only 1 among a thousand is enough to move the hand of God!'*

God does not always use an army of intercessors. He only needs one, just one among a thousand people! So next time you are urged in your heart to pray for someone just be available as a vessel that God can use. Even if you are that one vessel. One vessel is enough! You are enough!

*"But if an angel from heaven appears— a special messenger to intercede for a person and declare that he is upright— he will be gracious'*

When you are available to stand in the gap you become that messenger and that angel. It's not that a physical angel will always come down but you will be an 'extension of God's kingdom' and become that angel, you become a life saver and you become that intercessor!

Secondly, we need to declare them as righteous by the ransom that was already paid on their behalf

*"But if an angel from heaven appears— a special messenger to intercede for a person and* ***declare that he is righteous****"*

I am reminded of the Israelites in Egypt who were protected from the plague of the death of the first born. Israelites were told to sprinkle blood on their door posts and the angel of death did not come to their houses. The same principle applies. The blood of the lamb in Egypt speaks of the blood of Jesus which is a ransom for the sins of the world. If we pray for someone we should pray for the covering of the blood of Jesus upon them and therefore we should declare them forgiven and ransomed by this blood!

When God hears your prayer he will be gracious and give the command, *'Rescue him from the grave, for I have found a ransom for his life.'*

Once the command is given our life is protected and our health is restored.

Finally, we should stand in the gap boldly and audaciously knowing that God is able. We should also stand in the gap constantly and frequently. This is in keeping with the revelation that God is actually in the business of saving people from premature death! Why is this the case? Because premature deaths slow down the advancement of God's kingdom. As seen before in the story of Jesus and Moses, all of them would have had their purposes terminated had they been killed in infancy. Likewise, if we die before achieving our purposes in life, the purpose of God is aborted before it's time and denied the opportunity to bless his creation! Premature death is so evil for this reason and so God's business is to ensure that time and time again he delivers his people from this evil and this abomination!

*""Yes, God does these things again and again for people. He rescues them from the grave so they may enjoy the light of life."*

*Job 33:29-30 NLT*

Some versions of the Bible say God does this *'twice and even three times'* but this translation puts it well and sheds more light. God does this *'again and again'* meaning that he does it, *continually, whenever there is need and without limit!'* Simply put ..... *'it's God's business to deliver from premature death!'*

So if it's God's business....

why not pray boldly?

why not pray audaciously?

why not pray arrogantly and continuously for God to deliver?

Why not declare and say 'I will pray, I will be among the one in a thousand as often as God moves me to do so! God being my help!'

# 7

# Transition and transmission

Transition leads to the release of God's great blessings upon the lives of the next generation. When we study the lives of the patriarchs we see that Isaac and Jacob both released a blessing on their children before they died. This speaks of the spiritual need to bless your children in life and especially before you leave this world!

However, for Christians, the point at which we transition is the point at which the blessings that God has promised to us are literally 'passed on' to the next generation.

### *The blessing endures*

The blessings of the Lord are unlike curses in the manner they operate. God promises to punish and visit the sins of father's to the third and fourth generation! However the blessing of God is unlimited in it's operation and there are several scriptures that show this fact,

*"I lay the sins of the parents upon their children; the entire family is affected—even children in the third and fourth generations of those who reject*

*me. But I lavish unfailing love for a thousand generations on those who love me and obey my commands." Exodus 20:5-6 NLT*

*"Understand, therefore, that the Lord your God is indeed God. He is the faithful God who keeps his covenant for a thousand generations and lavishes his unfailing love on those who love him and obey his commands." Deuteronomy 7:9 NLT*

*"But the love of the Lord remains forever with those who fear him. His salvation extends to the children's children of those who are faithful to his covenant, of those who obey his commandments!" Psalms 103:17-18 NLT*

*""Tell Aaron and his sons to bless the people of Israel with this special blessing: 'May the Lord bless you and protect you. May the Lord smile on you and be gracious to you. May the Lord show you his favor and give you his peace.'"* "Whenever Aaron and his sons bless the people of Israel in my name, I myself will bless them."" Numbers 6:23-27 NLT

The blessings of God are seen, in these scriptures, culminating in the children of Israel but were first given to Abraham when God promised to bless him and make him a blessing to all people. Then, Isaac blessed Jacob and in turn Jacob blessed each of his twelve sons which became the twelve tribes of Israel. All these blessings passed on to the next generation at the point of birth of the next generation and also at the point of death of the older generation!

### Transition and judgment

One sad thing I see about the point of death is that it is point of both finality and judgement. Jacob did not only appropriate a blessing but he also appropriated God's judgment on two of his sons.

Reuben slept with his father's concubine and lost his birthright for this

*"Reuben, you are my firstborn, my strength, the child of my vigorous youth. You are first in rank and first in power. But you are as unruly as a flood, and you will be first no longer. For you went to bed with my wife; you defiled my marriage couch." Genesis 49:3-7 NLT*

Reuben lost his honor as first born due to the judgement that fell on him. A somewhat similar scenario happened to his two brothers,

*"Simeon and Levi are two of a kind; their weapons are instruments of violence. May I never join in their meetings; may I never be a party to their plans. For in their anger they murdered men, and they crippled oxen just for sport. A curse on their anger, for it is fierce; a curse on their wrath, for it is cruel. I will scatter them among the descendants of Jacob; I will disperse them throughout Israel." Genesis 49:3-7 NLT*

Simeon and Levi, slaughtered a whole city in vengeance for the rape of their sister, Dinah. This was done at a time when their father Jacob demonstrated a deep lesson of repentance when he, Jacob, knelt at the feet of Esau repenting dearly for stealing the blessing of the first born that came from their father Isaac. Simeon and Levi, saw that their uncle Esau forgave their father Jacob and with him, forgave the whole family including themselves. However shortly after this incident, as their family was settling after returning from he country of their grandfather Laban, they did not reciprocate the grace of forgiveness that they received.

When Shechem, the prince of King Hamor the Hivite, came to apologize for his error, and declare his genuine love for Dina, Simeon and Levi were obsessed with anger and tricked them in evil deceit. They schemed to incapacitate all the men by asking that they can only allow the marriage to their sister to be on condition that they are circumcised and with them all the men of their land. Due to Shechem's deep love for Dina, they agreed to do this. But alas, while the Hivite men were still in pain and incapacitated, Simeon and Levi took advantage of them and slew them with the sword! This anger and failure to forgive, and this cunning and deadly deceit brought a curse on their lives. You also will see that they never repented for their sin when rebuked by their father Jacob, on the contrary they defended themselves and never attempted to make peace with the Hivites for what they had done. Simply put, sin in general if unresolved and unconfessed brings a curse on people's lives.

We should always do our best to follow the command of scripture to 'make peace with all men as much as it is in our power to do so'.

Another example is the story of David and Solomon. At the point of death David has some unresolved hurts. People had done him wrong and he commanded that his son Solomon execute judgement on his enemies.

When you look at the prophetic role of Solomon you will end up agreeing with many bible scholars who describe him as a representation of, or a type of, Christ. In him God demonstrates many things that show how Christ himself will rule on earth as King for ever. Firstly he was the natural son of David, he was born from David's bloodline and became king fulfilling the prophecy of Isaiah 11:1-3, and then his reign was characterized by absolute peace and no wars at all for as long as his heart was fixed on God. He was endowed with divine wisdom and he was also a servant king. He was the son of Bathsheba the wife of a Hittite and this was prophetic in that though Hittites were a Gentile nation they were included in God's kingdom. Solomon's kingship confirms ancient prophecies which foretold that honor would come to the gentiles by their spiritual relationship to the Messiah.

David also had many sons, and many born before Solomon, yet Solomon was made the firstborn, higher than all the rest, and his father's heir and his brethren's prince; this is in fulfillment of the prophecy in Psalms 89:27,

*"I will make him my firstborn, higher than the kings of the earth."*

And is also in fulfillment of Psalms 45:7,

*"Thy God hath anointed thee with the oil of gladness above thy fellows'*

So Solomon is a type of Christ.... but what does this tell us and why am I emphasizing this point? Well I believe that at the point of death we should 'handover', as David did, all our hurts and pains to Jesus! Though David sought vengeance there is one thing we learn. He himself chose not to avenge. He also knew that the deep wisdom in his son would lead to his soul finding peace as his enemies are dealt with. History shows us another example were this principle applies. For example the blood of Abel is recorded to have cried out to God for his murder and untimely death by the his own brother's hand. So what we learn is that the sins done to the dead and dying are not rubbed off. They are now handled by Christ who ensures that they are avenged.

*"As the time of King David's death approached, he gave this charge to his son Solomon: "I am going where everyone on earth must someday go. Take courage and be a man.....*

*And there is something else. You know what Joab son of Zeruiah did to me when he murdered my two army commanders, Abner son of Ner and Amasa son of Jether. He pretended that it was an act of war, but it was done in a time of peace, staining his belt and sandals with innocent blood. Do with him what you think best, but don't let him grow old and go to his grave in peace. "Be kind to the sons of Barzillai of Gilead. Make them permanent guests at your table, for they took care of me when I fled from your brother Absalom. "And remember Shimei son of Gera, the man from Bahurim in Benjamin. He cursed me with a terrible curse as I was fleeing to Mahanaim. When he came down to meet me at the Jordan River, I swore by the Lord that I would not kill him. But that oath does not make him innocent. You are a wise man, and you will know how to arrange a bloody death for him. " Then David died and was buried with his ancestors in the City of David." 1 Kings 2:1-2, 5-10 NLT*

What we see from David's instruction is that,

*'Joab was not to grow old and die in peace because he murdered David's two army commanders in a time of peace!*

*'the sons of Barzillai of Gilead were to receive kindness and be permanent guests at Solomon's table because they took care of David when he was being pursued by his rebellious and murderous son Absalom, and*

*'Shimei was to receive a bloody death for cursing David!*

What I learn is that the wrong we do will have to be accounted for. Causing pain for no reason, or just in abuse of power and a simple show of force is a sin. It is evil and should not be tolerated, it brings premature death and you do not die in peace! If you mock and taunt God's anointed or disrespect authority or those that are anointed by God, you will be destroyed by the anointing and therefore God gave Shimei a bloody death of being struck by the sword in 2 Kings 1:46.

An interesting point to note is that when we choose to forgive people, their sins still remain in the eyes of God. It is like in law whereby you have criminal offenses and civil offenses. Civil offenses are usually between people. They make amends usually by retribution as much as possible and continue living their lives. Criminal offenses are offenses between the state and the offender. Usually these are serious crimes like murder or other grievous offenses. With these offenses, it is the state that takes responsibility to prosecute the offender and this is exactly what happened with David. He is leaving his hurts in the hands of Christ, the heavenly king who would execute justice on his behalf. David specifically said 'though I forgave him it does not mean he is without guilt' and this guilt will follow him.

This means that as Christians we should make it a point to make peace with all men before they or we die. In fact I believe we should learn from Zacheus who paid back 4 times what he stole from the poor. Though you may not have the capacity to repay 4 times at least repay what you have to repay to people. I believe that forgiveness by people itself does not absolve us from 'making good' the loss and pain we have caused.

It's better to repay on earth than to repay on the judgement day. Because God's principle is that you repay 4 times in other words you completely make good of not only the loss but the consequences too!

For this reason I believe a lot of Christians will loose so much on the judgement day, they will just enter heaven having worked for others because their business enterprise or other rewards from their service on earth has been allocated, credited and attributed to others in compensation for the wrongs done to them. Though they seemingly die rich, they will enter heaven as very poor people!

### *Kindness*

Another lesson we learn is the lesson of kindness. We see that because of simple kindness to David, the sons of Barzillai received permanent favor and were always in the kings presence. This means we should never underrate the kindness we do to people. God will repay! And at the point of transmission, the point of death, God's blessings will abound even if the people we helped were unable to repay us, God himself will see to it that your kindness is repaid! So go on and be kind, defend the weak, and be gracious to the poor and powerless! Because you are entreating the very kindness of God himself!

And in terms of being hurt in life, we see that Joseph was acquainted with suffering from an early age and received a fitting blessing from God, one that is almost greater than all his brothers combined!

""*Joseph is a fruitful bough, A fruitful bough by a well; His branches run over the wall. The archers have bitterly grieved him, Shot at him and hated him. But his bow remained in strength, And the arms of his hands were made strong By the hands of the Mighty God of Jacob (From there is the Shepherd, the Stone of Israel), By the God of your father who will help you, And by the Almighty who will bless you With blessings of heaven above, Blessings of the deep that lies beneath, Blessings of the breasts and of the womb. The blessings of your father Have excelled the blessings of my ancestors, Up to the utmost bound of the everlasting hills. They shall be on the head of Joseph, And on the crown of the head of him who was separate from his brothers." Genesis 49:22-26 NKJV*

When you look at the blessing of Joseph you see that he went through adversity but he is promised that, in spite of it all, he will be strengthened by his God! Even though he was rejected and separated by his very own brothers he will flourish. So I pray the same blessing upon you. The blessing of flourishing in adversity! And the blessing of unfair favor!

So when all is said and done, make sure you make peace while you are alive and also while your neighbor is alive, make peace before they die, when this happens you have a civil case you can easily resolve. If possible, don't just make peace by saying sorry.. no! You need to try to restore the loss and heal the pain of others, if you do not do so, your case will be handled by the state of heaven and it will be you and the state of heaven, you and the King of heaven. And believe you me, he is a righteous judge, and your judgement will surely come! So be at peace with all men as much as it is in your power to do so!

""*When you are on the way to court with your adversary, settle your differences quickly. Otherwise, your accuser may hand you over to the judge, who will hand you over to an officer, and you will be thrown into prison. And if that happens, you surely won't be free again until you have paid the last penny."* Matt 5:25-26 NLT

Remember...We are all on our way to the heavenly courts.

### *Transmission of the anointing*

The anointing is a marvelous gift that is given to various people in various measures. Such anointing also has the potential to transfer from one person to another. A good example of a powerful anointing was that of prophet Elijah who was called the prophet of fire!

He was fed three times with divine help. First by ravens at the brooch called Cherith, then by a widow in Zarephath and lastly by an angel from heaven!

He was a fearless prophet who rebuked kings, he was fervent and steadfast in prayer as seen in his praying for rain to cease for three years.

He caused rain to stop, raised a child from the dead, split waters of the mighty Jordan river, multiplied a meal and oil, called fire from heaven to consume a sacrifice, called fire from heaven to consume a whole battalion of soldiers and finally prayed for the rain to fall again after a three year drought!

Something unique happened between Elijah and his young apprentice Elisha. As Elisha was about to be taken away to heaven, Elijah tried to elude Elisha three times! But Elisha stuck to Elijah like a magnet! He was so persistent that finally Elijah granted Elisha one last request as his apprentice.

*'What shall I do to you before I am taken away?*

*I want a double portion of your anointing'*

Elijah was taken by a whirlwind but something remarkable happened to Elisha. The anointing that was on Elijah now rested on Elisha! In fact not only did it transfer but it was indeed a double portion on him.

Elisha went on to perform twice as many miracles and all with remarkable effect.

Elisha crosses the Jordan by splitting it in two by the mantle that fell from his master as he was taken up into heaven. Elisha cursed some boys who laughed at his boldness and they were mauled by two female bears. He cleaned the infected waters at Jericho, he multiplied the oil of a widow who was importuned by a harsh creditor. The oil was not only enough to pay off her debts but also to live on the rest!

Elisha prophesied that a barren Shunamite woman would bear a son. Later in life this same some child would die but Elisha would pray and resurrect the boy. Elisha purified poisonous food and fed 100 men with 20 loaves in a fashion similar to how Jesus fed the 5,000.

He cured the leprosy of a Syrian commander, Naaman, fully restoring the health of his skin to that of a little child! But... He punished his own servant who took gifts of money and clothing from Naaman. He repeatedly saved Israel's king Jehoram from enemy ambushes. He struck Arameam soldiers with blindness leading to their capture! he made and iron axehead float on water, he prophesied relief from Israel's enemies and the end of famine, he prophesied the kingship and death of King Hazael.

This guy was on a roll! He made Elijah's miracles look like child's play. He was so anointed it looked like the power and anointing within him was just looking for an opportunity to display God's glory. This guy was so anointed that he performed an amazing miracle even after his death! Talk of weird right? Can you imagine that Elisha's dry bones raised a dead man to life? The man was being buried but for fear of the army of Israel's enemies, he was simply thrown into Elisha's tomb and once his body touch the bones, the man came to life! That is just mind blowing! The guy was on steroids as far as miracles are conceded!

The anointing was transmitted from Elijah to Elisha and in a double portion at the time of Elisha's transition!

This repeats itself in the life of Jesus. Jesus said

*'the things I do you will do also and you will do them in greater measure!'*

So he promised his disciples the anointing and baptism of the Holy Spirit and 2000 years later the church is still performing miracles of all sorts.

What does this mean for us? I think it means that God still pursues the purposes of his kingdom through us if we remain faithful to build on the good work of our forerunners! I think even in the loss of our loved ones their spiritual gifting can still operate in us by God's grace. What we need is to serve the kingdom and serve with those who are anointed among us. And also to yearn for and share in the corporate anointing flowing from their lives.

We also ought to pray for God to establish in us the blessing even if you might be going through moments of uncertainty due to loss and a shakeup of your ministry or service to God! But God remains faithful. He will finish what he started even if others don't finish and, he will establish in-us the promises he made to our father's or to our leaders!

# 8

# Honoring those who transition

I deliberately wrote this chapter right after the passing of my Dad. I thought it appropriate because I have often heard of people talk of the futility of our efforts to honor the loved ones who have passed. Specifically in the way their bodies are taken care of.

As a result, you will hear people talk of the futility of donning their bodies in decent clothes, or of buying a decent coffin or of decently preparing their bodies to look presentable in appearance and so on. This is done all in the name of spirituality of course and of our desire for a new life in heaven. Well this is not quite right...

The story of Mother Teresa, I find to be quite intriguing. She established a hospice for the sick destitute and the dying. She converted a Hindu temple into a hospice that was initially called 'Mother Teresa's Kalighat Home for the Dying Destitutes' and as a result people received medical attention and an opportunity to die with dignity.

"*A beautiful death,*" she said,

"*is for people who lived like animals to die like angels—loved and wanted.*"

One other example of honoring those who transition is found in the Jewish tradition which is revealed on various occasions in the Bible. One of the most common Jewish rites was to wash the dead but also to anoint their bodies with oil and spices and to finally wrap their bodies in spices. The purpose of this was to prepare the body for its final resting place by a process of purification. Most cultures and religions have similar rites with several variations.

In the Jewish tradition they would recite words of prophecy as they performed the rites including the following;

*'I will sprinkle clean water on you, and you shall be clean from all your uncleannesses, and from all your idols I will cleanse you.' Ezekiel 36:25*

This would be done in faith that God is the one who purifies his people from their sin. In Acts 9:37 reference is also made to Dorcas whose body was washed when she died. Even medically this is something that happens by medical people who ensure that they clean and prepare the body for burial.

Jesus was also anointed but this happened before he died! Mary Magdalene brought an expensive box of alabaster to Jesus filled with expensive perfume and spices and she broke it on the feet of Jesus in deep and extreme devotion. It is believed that she is the woman who was caught in adultery and would have been stoned to death had it not been for Jesus. In fact the Pharisees protested to her even touching Jesus and said *'if you had known the type of woman touching you, you would not have allowed it!'* Essentially saying *'how can you be touched by a prostitute'.* Luke 7:36-50

But Jesus the great defender came to her defense yet again. He explained to her that what was happening was a spiritual thing and not at all physical.

Yes it was an act of devotion. An act of deep gratitude for not only being forgiven but also being given a second chance at life. She saw her life come to an end on that sinful and fateful day. But instead of being stoned to death Jesus was her defense! Jesus was her new lease of life!

Perhaps no one captures her emotion better that Cece Winans in her song titled 'Alabaster box'

*'And I've come to pour*

*My praise on Him like oil*
*From Mary's Alabaster Box*
*Don't be angry if I wash His feet with my tears*
*And I dry them with my hair*
*You weren't there the night He found me*
*You did not feel what I felt*
*When He wrapped His loving arms around me*
*And you don't know the cost*
*Of the oil in my Alabaster* box

In her grand and inexplicable gesture of gratitude, Jesus defended her yet again and said

*"Leave her alone. She did this in preparation for my burial." John 12:7 NLT.*

I just love these words of Jesus because it reveals to me a deep truth. It reveals that even God was interested in the last rites of Jesus body! Yes Jesus body was anointed before his death because God knew that the women would be too late to anoint his body. He would have already risen from the dead! And indeed the story is recounted that on the third day after Jesus's death the same Mary Magdalene sought to anoint the body of Jesus.

Now, I love this translation of the New Living Translation since it talks of why the anointing took place which is 'to prepare Jesus' body for burial'. Other versions mostly talk of the future reason which is to 'keep some of it for my burial' and indeed this was fulfilled as she sought to do so with the other women. She then was told that Jesus was risen and that she was too late. Fortunately, God in his wisdom had already allowed her to anoint the body of Jesus! Praise God!

Another good example of the importance of respecting our loved ones is well illustrated by Joseph of Aramethea.

You see... according to Roman tradition crucified criminals were often left on the cross to rot without a decent burial. The purpose was to quell any revolt and committing similar crimes, and to humiliate, torture, and kill criminals in clear view of the public.

It is widely accepted that criminals were never brought down from the cross at the request of family members etc. since bringing their bodies down from the cross for burial would defeat the whole purpose of crucifixion. Instead, they left criminals on the cross so the birds and dogs could devour their bodies. When nothing was left, their bones were taken down from the cross and not placed in nice burials, but tossed into places like Golgotha which rightly means the place of skulls.

It is against this background that Joseph of Arimathea did something remarkable and profound. He went against the norm and demanded the body of Jesus so it should not meet a criminal's fate!

He could not allow this to happen. Now, we need to know who Joseph was for us to appreciate the enormous challenge he had.

Joseph was mentioned by all four of the New Testament Gospel's. He is described as

*'A member of the Sanhedrin*

*'Who had become a disciple of Jesus*

*'A believer of Christ*

But John added one more detail... Joseph was indeed a disciple but he kept it a secret for fear of the Jews! Wow that is a big problem when you don't want the body of your Saviour to be hung on a cross until it rots! Until it's eaten by birds and dogs... that my friends is a big problem!

How do you ensure your master is properly buried without putting your life at risk? How do you remain safe when the Jews know that one of the key members of their own Sanhedrin, an organization whose very survival is at threat because of Jesus, so much so that this threat must be eliminated, is actually a disciple of Jesus? Joseph was not only in between a rock and hard place, he was fully in both places. To bury Jesus' body would be an open display of allegiance to him, to defy the wisdom logic and actions of the Sanhedrin in crucifying Jesus, to be rejected by them and throw his career to the dogs, and ultimately would be to request the same fate of his master to befall him. And perhaps this time no one would have the courage to deliver his body from rotting on the cross?

But upon hearing of Jesus' death, remarkably and with much personal danger, this secret disciple of Jesus went to Pilate and requested the body of Jesus. Pilate gave him permission, giving him a letter and decree in his own seal which, I imagine, read something like this;

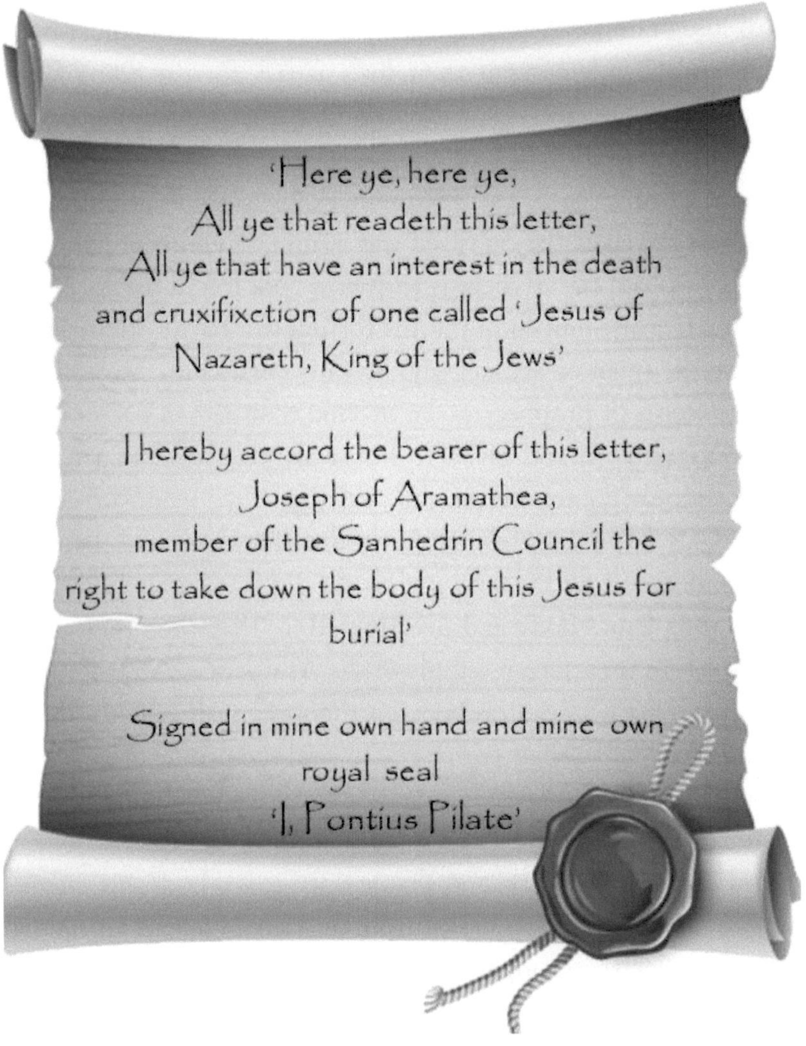

'Here ye, here ye,
All ye that readeth this letter,
All ye that have an interest in the death
and cruxifixction of one called 'Jesus of
Nazareth, King of the Jews'

I hereby accord the bearer of this letter,
Joseph of Aramathea,
member of the Sanhedrin Council the
right to take down the body of this Jesus for
burial'

Signed in mine own hand and mine own
royal seal
'I, Pontius Pilate'

That was all he needed!, just one page of a scroll, not too long, but just enough to keep the Roman guards on Golgotha at bay. They would come snarling like wolves but at the sight of the letter bearing Pilate's seal, written in his own hand, Joseph would walk right through them to collect the body of his master from the cross.

He was joined by another secret disciple, Nicodemus and they bought spices and proceeded to wrap his body with linen clothes and the spices. Then they buried Jesus in a tomb that is believed to have belonged to Joseph himself! Wow! What sacrifice and what dedication!

Joseph and Nicodemus put their lives at risk for the sake of their beloved master. There are too or three similar stories of similar dedication and purpose. Mark 15:42-47

The first is Saul's death. There is a remarkable story that tells of how Saul's soldiers retrieved the captured and humiliated body of King Saul.

The story of Saul's death begins with how Saul fell in battle. He had first consulted a medium to tell of his fortunes in battle. The medium conjured up the spirit of Samuel who literally curses him again by confirming the words of prophecy given by God that he had been rejected and his kingdom torn and given to his rival David. On hearing this, the battle did not go any better the next day. They were surrounded and he and his three sons fell by the sword that day. Soul, being severely wounded, fell on his own sword. As did his amour bearer. The Philistines took Saul's body and decapitated it. They then took his armor and put it in their pagan temple of the Ashtoreths as a trophy!

They then hung his headless body on their city wall in Beth-Shan as a prize and mockery to their sworn enemy and the people of Israel.

But something remarkable happened. There were Israelite warriors in a small town who heard of Saul's death and the fate that befell him, they heard of the humiliation and shame done to his body, his memory and his honor. These warriors hailed from the City of Jabesh Gilead. The Bible records that these mighty warriors were infuriated about what had been done to Saul and set to restore his honor.

Each and every one of them took up arms and decided to leave that very evening, riding their horses throughout the night with the singular intention of retrieving the bodies of their king and his family. They not only marched all night but also had to cross the mighty Jordan river.

They arrived in Beth Shan and retrieved Saul's headless body and the impaled bodies of his princes. They mounted them on their horses and brought them back to Jabesh in the land of Israel for a decent burial. So these mighty men performed the burial rites of washing and anointing them with oil. Then they cremated their bodies and buried their bones. The men of Jabesh-Gilead had finally given their king an honorable burial. A burial fit for royalty. (1 Samuel 31)

This was a valorous act, a complete show of not only valor but also of dedication! But what fueled this audacity! The story of Saul's burial actually started in the beginning of Saul's kingship and is recorded in 1 Samuel 11, where the Ammonite King Nahash attacked the town Jabesh Gilead.

It is said that the Ammonites were so sadistic that the only peace treaty acceptable to Nahash was that he gouge out one eye from each man of Jabesh.

During the week of deliberations they requested help from Saul, who was then the newly crowned king. Saul mustered the forces of Israel at Bezek, marched all night, attacked Nahash early in the morning, and by noon had the enemy scattered. Because of this, Saul gained the allegiance of Jabesh-gilead and all trans-jordan.

The kindness of Saul, the valor of Saul, his commitment to his subjects and allegiance to his people, followed him and reciprocated even in his death.

Saul was touched and responded to the plight of Jabesh. The men of Jabesh were also touched with the plight of their king! They were the only ones who responded with such speed, not one mighty warrior or any part of Israel achieved this magnanimous feat. And no one in all of Israel responded, even though all of Israel had been equally humiliated by the desecration of their king's body.

It's exactly what Goliath did. He cursed the God and nation of Israel on the battle field. He called out one man from Israel to have the guts to fight him. And David, then a mere shepherded boy, was infuriated by the humiliation of Israel and their new king Saul, similarly the men of Jabesh-Gilead were infuriated that their king was hung on a wall.

The shepherd boy asked who '*defies the armies of Israel and the armies of the living God?*'

Saul's anger in fact was so furious that when he heard of the message from Nahash he stopped plowing his field, killed his two oxen and sent pieces of them throughout all Israel. Saul vowed in holy anger that

*'this fate will befall all your oxen if you refuse to join me in battle against Nahash'*

Saul's anger was God inspired because the Bible records that

*"the Spirit of God came powerfully upon Saul, and he became very angry." 1 Samuel 11:6 NLT*

And indeed God made the people so afraid of this holy anger that they all came out as one. And 600,000 warriors were mustered that day!

I believe it is the same holy anger that God put in the men of Jabesh-Gilead that led them to rescue Saul's body from the Philistines.

Saul marched all night and arrived in Jabesh Gilead before dawn! And annihilated his enemies! And in similar fashion the men of Jabesh-Gilead marched all night and rescued their king! These mighty men put their lives in danger of attack but prevailed and retrieved the bodies of their master and his sons! What a feat! What an honor!

Do we understand what this act was to the Gileadites?

It was a show of allegiance to their king and his reputation. It was a show of patriotism and allegiance to their nation and even to their God who had blessed their nation with this first king.

It was a show of Holy Ghost inspired anger!

It was a show of gratitude to the only man who defended them in the heat of battle and to whom they literally owed their lives!

The crux of the matter is that it was a show of complete devotion to their slain master. A deep devotion of a grateful and thankful heart for what God had done to them in their darkest hour. The result of this was a blessing from both God and David the new king,

*"And David sent messengers unto the men of Jabesh-gilead, and said unto them, Blessed be ye of Jehovah, that ye have showed this kindness unto your lord, even unto Saul, and have buried him. And now Jehovah show lovingkindness and truth unto you: and I also will requite you this kindness, because ye have done this thing."* 2 Samuel 2:5-6 ASV

There is also a story of a curse that God gave to one king who had not pleased him. I am fascinated by this story of King Jeroboam. He was so wicked before God in his idol worship that he actually did more evil than all the Kings before him! For this, God said he will destroy his kingdom and his household and that his household will not be buried. If they died in the city, the dogs would eat them, if in the country then the birds of the air would eat them. This same curse came to Ahab and Jezebel for their wicked acts too. And the Bible records that this happened for these two. (1 kings 14, 18,19)

So it seems that God considered the lack of a proper burial as a punishment to wicked people.

For those of us who have had the honor of burying our parents we ought to think of Ecclesiastes 6:3 which talks of the futility of those who have children that cannot even accord them a decent burial.

*"If a man beget a hundred children, and live many years, so that the days of his years are many, but his soul be not filled with good, and moreover he have no burial; I say, that an untimely birth is better than he:" Ecclesiastes 6:3 ASV*

The message of this verse for me is that God expects you to honor your father's and loved ones even in their death, last rites and burial.

The next story I like is the story of Moses's burial. The Bible records that God himself buried him! Imagine that, imagine God doing the honors of burial? Indeed what an honor, what does this teach us? Well several things I believe.

First, God is concerned about how you are treated when you transition just as he was concerned and even prepared Jesus' body for burial.

The honor you give to your loved ones is an act of devotion and appreciation to who they are and what they have been to you! Mary anointed Jesus because of the forgiveness and new lease of life she received from Jesus.

Saul received honor from the warriors of Jabesh because they were grateful for what Saul had done to them in his life.

Yahweh himself honored Moses by burying him personally, wow! So next time you hear some 'spiritual' people dismissing the memory of your loved ones, please remember the stories of love and devotion that we find all through the Bible. And remember to do your best. Not to over burden yourself or to be a show of opulence and abundance but indeed to be a show of love and of celebration for the gift of their lives, the guidance and blessings that God channeled through them and as praise to God for his goodness and the opportunity and sheer privilege of being in their lives and of them being so close and dear to us! Remember that there is a blessing for such loyalty!

*"And David sent messengers unto the men of Jabesh-gilead, and said unto them, Blessed be ye of Jehovah, that ye have showed this kindness unto your lord, even unto Saul, and have buried him. And now Jehovah show lovingkindness and truth unto you: and I also will requite you this kindness, because ye have done this thing."* 2 Samuel 2:5-6 ASV

May God help you to honor your loved ones and also the memory of your loved ones, to the extent that he has enabled you or is able to provide for you... Amen!

*Acts that honor our loved ones*

I think there is no one way of honoring our loved ones. I believe it mostly depends on culture, faith and also the relationship you have had with them in life. Practically for me this meant that together with my family we did our best to cherish the memory of our dad and give him a decent send off and funeral that left us with fond memories of him. Fortunately we had a medical policy for him that also catered somewhat to funeral expenses and for some of us this may mean having something similar or making arrangements to ensure that in the event of loss of your loved ones you able to at least meet some immediate and basic costs, or it may mean that perhaps you plan for a funeral policy or similar arrangements. Whatever you do to support your family in life and in death you do it to honor them and and as an expression of your love for them and of thankfulness to God for them.

# 9

# Mourning those who transition

I am no psychiatrist who can sit you down with an expert methodology of how to bring emotional healing. I am only someone who has himself suffered the deep pain of loss like many others who have suffered loss and who inevitably will suffer loss as we journey through life.

Grieving is a process that I find to be rather complex. Grieving is all about being sad and sorrowful on the loss of our loved ones. The way we all grieve is definitely unique to ourselves and definitely dissimilar to how anyone else would grieve, simply because we are different.

Grieving is also a challenge because of how we all understand it and how we understand death in very different ways. Once again, I think those of us who are spiritual are at risk of mishandling grief and the people that grieve.

The other category of people who can make these mistakes is those who have not experienced loss. To be honest we are human and in our humanness we share in the pain of others. But there is some pain that may never be understood until we encounter it first hand in some degree or form.

What I mostly see people do is to dismiss the grief, pain and worry of the bereaved with some encouraging words. They will tell you 'be strong!, don't cry because the family will see you cry, or the kids will see you or your spouse will see you cry !'

If they see you mourning they will literally or practically stop you dead in your tracks in order for you to 'be strong'.

If you talk of your ordeal, others will stop you and replace your lamenting with a scripture.

Personally, I think all these are well intentioned, there are more moments in which we need to be strong. I remember how these words encouraged me in my loss because they were indeed well intended. In my bewildered state of mind I was encouraged to pull through and fight on. I was able to garner the last bits of strength to help me make sense of the chaos. But, I believe, there is more we can do to understand those who mourn. And to avoid the same words of encouragement becoming a tool that bottles up emotion and to delay healing.

The human spirit is complex and unique, and it quickly senses the spirit in which anything is done. It is therefore vital to ensure that all encouragement is given in a spirit of love and not legalism. You can sense when encouragement is coming in love because the words 'be strong' will mean 'fight on' 'God is with you' 'you are not alone!' However, if the spirit of love is missing, all encouragement will come in a manner that misses the point. It will be about

*'you are breaking protocol'*

*that's not how it should be done so be strong,'*

*'don't cry' is no longer 'don't despair' it becomes*

*'why are you crying?'*

*'This is not the time to cry'.*

*'You can cry later'.*

Or, like Elisha's Servant we will say *'Don't cry in the presence of the prophet!'*

*'You are not creating an atmosphere for the presence of God and the miraculous'*

As you can imagine it's quite complex to give comfort right? It truly is but at the same time it's about the heart and spirit of love from which we reach out.

One simple thing to do is to simply share your company. This is a powerful encouragement in the grieving process because you are at little risk of misapplying any theology and all you do is show your solidarity to them. Job's friends were better encouragers and consolers when they remained silent during the first 7 days than they ever where when they opened their mouths.

This approach of just giving company is therapeutic because you allow yourself to have a unique perspective of comforting others. You start understanding that life is about showing love and solidarity. So even though someone may not be ready to deal with it today you will stand with him until he is ready.

Sharing your company let's the person who is grieving grieve at his own pace. They may open up to you and slowly let out their pain. It also allows them to reminisce and talk fondly of those who have died. I think this also helps you to heal because you are now able to mention your loved ones and not treat them as a taboo topic that must never be mentioned. You start talking of their humor, the funny little things they used to do, what you miss most about them and so on. Talking about them may not be to the same degree with everyone but at least you are able to talk about hopes for the future, business or work.

This also helps because mostly those who grieve experience what I call 'comfort overload' or 'preaching overload'. It is natural for comforters to preach God's word as they attempt to encourage you. But the fact is that you will receive a lot of this preaching. Some will be encouraging and effective and some less so, because of the mode of delivery, their knowledge of God's word and simply your emotional state among other relevant factors. So simply chatting with someone and saying bye can be a powerful encouragement and aide in the grieving process too.

There are several reasons why we mourn and the Bible has several examples of why it is healthy to mourn. The first reason simply comes from the definition of grieving itself. We mourn and grieve simply because we are reacting to fond memories of our loved ones. We miss who they were to us and how important they have proved themselves to be towards us. That's why we mourn. There is nothing wrong in that! You have someone who loved you and you miss them. Naturally you will miss them. When you remember their role in life, the things they did for you and the family, and their duty bound commitment you really feel the gaps they have left in life.

No matter how spiritual we may be surely there is nothing wrong in this!

The Bible has several examples of people who mourned in times of death. I am reminded of Jonathan who together with his father Saul was mourned poetically and expertly by David. First of all, David tore his clothes as did all his men! Then he mourned the whole day and fasted. He later lamented and sang a sad song

*"Oh, how the mighty heroes have fallen in battle! Jonathan lies dead on the hills. How I weep for you, my brother Jonathan! Oh, how much I loved you! And your love for me was deep, deeper than the love of women! Oh, how the mighty heroes have fallen! Stripped of their weapons, they lie dead."* 2 Samuel *1:25-27 NLT*

I also recall Jesus of whom the Bible says was heart broken at the death of his friend Lazarus but more so, at the grief of Mary and Martha who fell at his feet and said *'if you had been here my brother would not have died'*. Sharing in their pain and looking at the crowd weeping and wailing, his heart was torn in two and the Bible simple records that *'Jesus wept'*!

If we return to the story of the Shunamite woman, prophet Elisha allowed her to mourn with much lamenting. In her confusion she made the point that the child who had died was not something she had asked from God by pestering and much prayer in the first place. She had accepted her fate and her barrenness. It was God's own prerogative to give her a child. Why would God put her through the pain of an emotional roller coaster ride? Why would he give her a gift she never dreamed of having, only to take it away again?

This woman identifies with all of us who grieve. She tells us that we all have questions that confuse us. I think in our mourning we ought to process our confusion. I think this is important because 'our confusion is the source of our pain'. If we don't process this confusion, the pain remains. It does not mean that we will get all the answers, far from it! But at least we acknowledge the source and 'the why' of our pain. And as the darkness lifts and the horizon get less blurry we are able to sort through the questions.

*We know which questions caused us pain,*
*Which questions have answers so far,*
*Which questions can still be answered and*
*Which questions to let go!*

That is the process I had to go through, but I had to process the pain of each loss I experienced. When my sister died I asked why we all missed the diagnosis until the very end, I lamented the missed diagnosis and higher chances of her recovery had we known what she was ailed with, which only came late in her treatment, I wondered what more I would, should and could have done in order to save her life! That was the source of my pain and those were the questions I had to sift through and come to terms with!

When my wife died three years later, I was basically stunned! It was so sudden and so traumatic. A head on collision with a drunk driver in a small truck swerved from his lane straight into ours. I always ask myself what else I would, could and should have done.

Should I have ran over the motorcyclist who also abruptly entered the road? because this to me contributed to my wife's death as I tried to avoid running him over by swerving away from him and getting into the road.

Should I have stopped suddenly or should I have seen this truck in time?

Should I even have gone on this trip in the first place?

Should I have prayed more? But since we all, as a church evangelism team, fasted and prayed in the week for this trip, should I have gone an extra mile?

Why would an accident happen when our prayer points specifically included praying against accidents in the first place?

Did God not hear our prayer?

Did we pray amiss?

The truth of the matter is that I may never find the answers to these questions. Because all I know is that we did what we ought to have done, we prayed, we fasted, we volunteered to go to an evangelism program because it is what we both loved and the accident happened and I can only believe that this did not take God by surprise.

Another element of processing your questions was when I had to answer my son's questions. Barely five years old, he could not understand what had happened and where mommy was. All he knew was that mommy promised him a milkshake on her return. I got a barrage of questions from him. And our conversation went like this

*Where is mommy?*

*She is in heaven*

*What is she doing there?*

*She is with Jesus*

*When is mommy coming back from heaven?*

*When we go to heaven we don't come back sweetie we will find her in heaven*

*I also want to go to heaven to be with mommy, when are we going to heaven?*

*We go to heaven when Jesus calls us we can not go on our own and you need to grow up first ok baby!*

*How do you get to heaven?*

*Angels carry us when Jesus calls us.*

I honestly, could not bring myself to tell my dear Sean that his mommy had died. I thought he did not understand the concept. But boy was I wrong! One day, out of the blue, he asked

*'Did mommy die?*

*I knew he has heard this from somewhere.*

*'Yes baby, she died.*

At my response he cried uncontrollably. I took him in my arms and said don't worry she is with Jesus. When we die we go to Jesus so don't worry ok. Then reality hit him....

*When I go to heaven will I also die?*

*Yes baby we all die when we go to heaven*

*But I don't want to die!*

*It's ok baby, Jesus wakes us up ok so don't worry about dying*

*So if mommy is in heaven who will be my mommy?*

*God will give you another mommy one day ok?*

*Ok daddy*

All I could tell him was that he is not alone and he will be with me. And I miss mommy too.

These questions are only part of the questions I got from Sean and also over a period of about three months. They wrenched me to the core, Sean drew emotions from deep within me as he forced me to face raw emotions hidden deep within me and himself.

However, I discovered that as you process your emotions you heal. As you help others in your family circle or circle of friends you also heal. You have to grieve and process your grief. If you feel like crying, cry! Don't hide your pain. I was sometimes in tears when I answered Sean's questions. I told him '*I am also sad. It it's ok you're not alone my baby, you're not alone.*'

It's important for kids to know that you share their pain. It's not always about being emotionally cold or strong but also that you share their pain and loss. They then learn that it is ok to grieve.

When dealing with the recent passing of my Dad, all I could say to myself was

*'a dagger has pierced my heart, a dagger concealed and what we thought was helping him medically seemed to seal his death.*

Now, why am I sharing all this? Not because I think I handled each situation perfectly or answered my son perfectly but because it tells of the humanness and reality of the the grieving process. The unanswered questions and the point of acceptance to which we should arrive sooner rather than later.

So all I can say on this is

'process your questions and come to terms with them'.

## *Types of grief*

As said before, people grieve differently. I was privileged to get a deeper understanding of this when i was being consoled by a dear pastor whom I respect as a father in the Lord, Mr Distone Chiweza. He invited me into his home following the death of my wife and took me through the scriptures and talked of how to handle grief. I will share with you some of the things he poured into my life in my own words as best as I understood them in addition to my own thoughts on this.

Grieving is largely dependent on your personality, and perhaps a bit of maturity, and in my view and experience with life. There is a ***sharp rise and sharp fall*** emotional personality, followed by ***sharp rise plateau and sharp fall*** emotional personality, then we have the ***gentle rise and gentle fall*** and then we have the ***gentle rise, plateau and gentle fall*** personalities.

## *Sharp rise, sharp fall*

Sharp risers and fallers are a volatile group of people. On hearing the news of loss, they immediately react, and they react very openly without hiding their grief. They can be dramatic and loud, visibly distraught and perhaps unable to effectively function. When you look at them, you would be concerned of whether, they will make it at all in life after this loss. But lo and behold, as quickly as they rose emotionally they also fall. I believe this group's falling is not a bad thing, in the grieving process we must all fall or emotionally settle because at that point we can move on and confront life again. I will call the fall as the healing and acceptance phase of grieving.

I think this happens quickly for this group because they have ably released their emotion and felt their pain. They shed their tears and let out all emotions regarding how deeply they have been hurt. They deal with the shock of the loss, they overcome emotions of denial and anger, and they finally accept the situation. They are then able to quickly heal.

## *Sharp rise, plateau, sharp fall*

This group of people are just a version of the sharp risers. They quickly show their grief, but get stuck at the peak of sorrow following their loss. I believe the plateau is an area of deep pain. It is a state of emotional trauma that you wrestle to overcome. It's almost an emotional prison from which you need to be released. The enemy that is being wrestled is anger and denial. We have questions of why this has happened, in the manner it has happened and at the time it has happened and to whom it has happened. Perhaps they were such, good people, warm people, spiritual people, diligent people or exemplary people. Why them and why someone close to you? The questions keep rolling in but as indicated before, we need to ask the questions and come to terms with them. Eventually we come to terms and, as a sharp riser, coming to terms helps you to quickly heal just as the sharp risers and fallers.

## *Gentle rise and fall*

Gentle risers and fallers, are not as fast as the sharp risers and fallers. These guys take time to move through all the stages described above from dealing with shock to acceptance and also to expressing their emotions. The grief builds up over time, and reaches its height well after the sharp risers and fallers. I think this can even be after the funeral has taken place. Or at least it can peak at the funeral since the funeral scene can unlock deep emotion for example as you see people mourning and especially as final rites are pronounced, the coffin is lowered, and perhaps buried in your presence. All this can cause deep emotion and cause you to peak. But even so, you can continue to peak after the funeral. As gently as you rise, it may equally take you a bit of time to heal. This happens gradually as you move to acceptance of the loss. But gradually you heal. The rationalization of what has happened, sorting through confusion, statements such as saying 'if only, if only' and sometimes trying to think of alternatives causes the delay in peaking but only when you accept reality can you heal.

### *Gentle rise, plateau and gentle fall*

This group of people are like the gentle risers and fallers however they get stuck on the peak of their grief. This group is the one that takes the longest time to move through all the stages of grieving from shock to acceptance and moving on. They do not sharply react but once the reality and impact of the loss hits them, it takes them time to come to terms. And they slowly move to a point where they accept it but due to their nature they then gradually heal, accept and move on.

### *Doorways of grief*

Grief comes about as a natural outcome of our fondness of loved ones. It is not a demon as some would believe. However when it comes we need to come to terms with it and heal. There are other types of grief that are triggered in an unwholesome manner and such must be guarded against. We need to ensure that we deal with friends who have lost loved ones, in a wholesome way and not in a way that literally torments them.

### *Guilt*

As said before, emotions of guilt can overwhelm us as we try to come to terms with loss. We naturally want to feel responsible for the shortcomings we thought could have been avoided. For example kids feel death happened because they were naughty, and so on and so forth. We need to know that death comes to all of us and that everything happens in its own time.

God says that not even a sparrow can fall without him knowing how much more important is a human life? God certainly cares and certainly knows! We should therefore prayerfully accept and be released from such unhealthy guilt (Mathew 10:9).

### *Careless talk*

When death happens, everyone usually has got something to say. This can be a dangerous practice especially for those who are not well informed of the events leading to the loss and are not as mature as others. They can speak irresponsible things to you that assign blame to you and how you should have done better.

### *Wrong spiritual interpretation*

The worst thing you can have is what I personally call a 'Holy Ignorant'. A holy ignorant is someone who talks holy, walks holy and thinks holy but unfortunately they are largely ignorant of why God allows death. These can break you because in addition to careless talk they back it up with the holy scriptures. This can be emotionally devastating and many people have been destroyed by such talkers. These people come to you, bible, in their hand, and say such painful things as you should have prayed more, you were weak in faith, you are being punished by God, you were not doing good works or did not pay your tithe and so on and so forth.

As much as possible let's ensure that we overcome and help others overcome guilt and unnecessary anguish by avoiding careless talk and uninformed words to others.

The most important thing to do is to know yourself and help yourself quickly come to the point of acceptance of the loss so you can quickly heal.

### *Free to grieve*

A proper understanding of grief helps you to permit yourself to grieve. Grieving is God's natural way of healing you and releasing the pain. Grief is important to all grieving personality types. The difference between the personality types is really the speed at which you move from shock, disbelief and anger to acceptance of the situation, and eventually forging ahead with life.

Now, speed is controlled by acceleration and deceleration. In a car, this is controlled by the gas pedal and the brake pedal. In our personality types the gas pedal is the emotions of sadness that overcome us. Our ability to accelerate through the grieving cycle helps us come to the end of the cycle and heal faster.

Inability to move through the cycle makes us stuck at various stages of it hence the common features of the various personality types.

Grieving is therefore clearly important to help you unleash your emotions to go through the cycle.

What affects grieving is the attempt to be strong and this results in the bottling up of emotions which then acts as a decelerator that slows down your grieving. Wrong theology by holy ignorants is also a decelerant as they will mostly ask you not to 'grieve as unbelievers' when in fact they are asking you not to grieve at all.

If there is something we should take home from our discussion on grief it's that it is healthy and especially so with hope in God. Paul talks about this in the following scripture

*"Now we do not want you to be uninformed, believers, about those who are asleep [in death], so that you will not grieve [for them] as the others do who have no hope [beyond this present life]. For if we believe that Jesus died and rose again [as in fact He did], even so God [in this same way—by raising them from the dead] will bring with Him those [believers] who have fallen asleep in Jesus." (AMP)" 1 Thessalonians 4:13-14*

Paul says there are two types of grieving, grieving of believers and grieving of non believers. The difference is clear, non believers have no hope beyond this present life but believers have hope beyond this life!

However one thing is clear, both are grieving! Therefore hoping in God doesn't mean 'not grieving' it means 'grieving but in hope'. *Grieving in hope* naturally starts with grieving. So if both are grieving why do we misinterpret this scripture and say that Christians should not grieve at all? I think this is a dangerous and harmful misinterpretation of scripture because it is unhealthy with negative spiritual, physical and emotional effects.

### *Bringing ourselves to grieve*

If 'grieving in hope' starts with 'grieving', duhh! ... Then we must grieve and must bring our self to grieve. But how can we do this, I think it's important to face reality and deliberately bring ourselves to grieve.

This is done by doing something that helps you remember and celebrate our loved ones. This can be through looking through photos and videos of our loved ones. If you are a slow riser who plateaus and slowly falls you may need to push yourself to do this and perhaps to watch funeral procession videos of your loved ones. You may need to talk about what has hurt you most on the loss of your loved one so you can come to terms with it and you come to the point of unlocking those healing emotions of grief.

We don't avoid grief by burying their memory or making them a taboo subject. We heal by talking about them, laughing as we talk about them, and cherishing the sheer gift they were to us.

That is how we heal and quickly accelerate from the despair of loss, confusion and anger, to the healing that that comes with hope that God is in control, God has our loved ones in his hands and that we will see them again one day in heaven. My prayer is that all of us who have experienced loss will allow and bring ourselves to grieve and to grieve like a believer!

# 10

# Raw emotion and allowing to be comforted

Transition of loved ones leads to very real and raw emotions that can sometimes make it difficult to be comforted. And sometimes we don't allow ourselves to be comforted because of the depth of our pain. We hold on to the pain for various reasons, some of which are valid. This chapter seeks to look into how we can still allow ourselves to be comforted and why this choice can prove beneficial while still allowing ourselves to grieve for our loved ones. A sort of win win situation...

## *Raw emotion and human comfort*

Man is inevitably limited in his capability to touch and heal hearts. I think it is important to understand that man's comfort comes to us within the confines of such limitations. In the midst of our limitations, however, we reach out to others due to our sense of responsibility and our natural caring nature for others. We make good attempts to condole a bereaved and saddened friend but some of which are less effective. Due to the pain, however, there is a possibility that we may misunderstand our friends or that we respond to them in a passively aggressive manner.

Let's discuss the raw emotions that can be felt and their impact on those being consoled. Finally we will see how we can surmount those challenges. These raw emotions are usually experienced when others are reaching out with comforting words such as those we discuss further in the following paragraphs.

***'On the demise of your loved one ....'*** is a common phrase. However this word literally means *'the end of all things'* and for someone who knows the word, this can conjure up thoughts of a permanent and hopeless loss. I think it's a normal way of condoling someone but in the heat of the moment it may be misunderstood and can emphasize hopelessness in those we console. So, we ought to understand the the spirit in which the words are said.

***'He is resting'*** can be dismissed and despised as being 'unreal' because others have thought death is totally different from the resting they would do in their bedroom or favorite couch and as a result may take offense in the heat of pain. The Bible however talks of resting, and we need to understand it from that perspective. Sometimes people will go through a lot of trouble in life or fight many battles including illness or will have lived a dedicated life of gallant service to their country and generations for a long time. At the end of all this the words 'resting' will indeed characterize a rest from all their labors, the illnesses and battles.

***'He is in a better place'*** can be thought of as presumptuous especially for secular people who don't believe in God or heaven. 'How can you know this?' most people think and if anyone where to know should it not be the bereaved who were closer to the deceased?

***'He was old' 'he was full of years' 'he was aged'*** can deeply rile your emotions because age and grief do not have a direct correlation. This assumes grief is felt less for the aged and more for the young. However this too is a false assumption. It's not about age it's about love, fondness and affection for our loved one! If this must be said it should said in a spirit of gratefulness for the long life that was granted by God not as a reason not to mourn them!

***'It has happened so just accept it'*** this is 'too logically correct' that it can almost seem heartless. It is true that it has happened but sometimes we have to understand why things happened in order to get closure. Sometimes, in order to avoid something we need to understand the causes that may unknowingly recur so we grow in wisdom from it. It is important to balance between denial and curiosity, denial and a sense of responsibility and accountability. That is why 'cause of death' is always critical in every loss and this is why postmortems are done to help explain to people why exactly their loved ones died.

***'It has happened so just celebrate his life'*** this can again conjure up feelings of permanence but is mostly well intended.

***'Read this verse or that verse'*** Sometimes, actually, most times, you will be battling with God as you may be thinking, he is unloving and uncaring. That he has allowed a bad thing to happen and that all the prayers have not been answered at all and your faith dishonored. You usually think God is not real. And or feel forsaken by him. Not everyone will understand the Bible during this time and few will be reading it if at all. I think the answer to this puzzle is to simply read the verse to them and encourage them as opposed to giving them homework or sending them on an errand. It's probably fine to say 'I am encouraged by this scripture and I hope it can encourage you too, if you have a moment you can look it up at your own time'.

***'I feel your pain'*** 'no you don't!' Is the common reaction... because all situations are different and it's not practically possible for someone to feel your pain. They may have experienced what your going through but everything is different.

You may also be consoled by those who have never experienced loss or your type of loss at least. This can cause you to say to yourself

'you don't what you're talking about'

'you don't know how I feel'

'it's easy for you to say this because you have no idea of what I'm going through'.

This may be true, but is largely unfair to those who are reaching out to us and we simply need to give people the benefit of the doubt. We need to let people reach out in the best way they can.

### *Choosing to see the good in people*

Grief can and is often mixed with bitterness, anger and even regret. This is a dangerous mix of emotions that can cause us all to be irrational, inhospitable and inconsolable at times. This is why well meaning statements such as those discussed above can be easily misunderstood and misinterpreted, and mostly unintentionally. I am sure when you say these words they are always well intentioned, it would not only be shocking but deeply hurtful if someone were to say their thoughts or respond verbally to your condolence.

*"A voice was heard in Ramah, weeping and loud lamentation, Rachel weeping for her children; she refused to be comforted, because they are no more." Matthew 2:18*

This is a description of the pain and sorrow of mothers and fathers in Bethlehem after King Herod had slain all the two year olds and under two year olds.

This shows us that firstly, the pain was too much for every household that had a two year old and under! We cannot discount the pain. But in the midst of the pain a choice was made....

*'I refuse consolation....'*

*Why?*

*'Because my children are no more'*

Was this a good or a bad choice! Well I think it was a necessary choice. Reverting to the Shunemite woman who mourned her son, the prophet said 'leave her be'.

Whether good or bad, sometimes raw emotion is good for us to process our grief! I am pretty sure the mothers of Bethlehem refused to be comforted as they saw their babies killed, ripped and torn apart by the sword. But it remains true that after a while, they had to move on. 'Move on' does not mean 'forget!' Move on means, in my view, *'choosing not to destroy yourself further because of the pain you have experienced'*.

I am sure the mothers remembered their toddlers for the rest of their lives, but this sorrow should not have deprived their future children of the love they were to show them. When they had other children they were not to emotionally abandon them because they were mourning their slain two year olds. That's a dangerous strategy and deprives the love to the people and children that are currently in your life.

Just as a conscious decision is made *'not to be consoled'* another must be made *'to live life'* .... and to live it *'as it should be lived'*. Lived with love to remaining family, with care and responsibility for what remains and with purpose amidst the confusion.

I think this level of maturity needs to be employed with raw emotion. We must make a conscious decision to understand human frailties and limitations. To understand that people have different limitations, maturity, theology and personalities. But, most of all, to understand that they too are human and they too are simply trying to reach out with a caring heart.

An over emphasis on what each of their words mean or the lack thereof is definitely not the most constructive use of your time or application of your thoughts, energies and emotions. People are simply human after all! So let them reach out to you in the best way they know how. To overemphasize on this is exactly what causes some people to shy away and stay away. We can't expect everyone to be picture perfect. No not at all!

Most people who know they have nothing to say or who think the person experiencing loss is higher in status than them, or is more knowledgeable than them tend to run away because they may feel inadequate and ill equipped to comfort them.

How do you comfort your pastor, deacon or church elder for example? How do you comfort your boss?

These are the challenges that even our friends face. We should not underestimate the care that others have for us. The fact that they have not experienced your exact form of pain does not mean they don't care. The very fact that they know you, are close to you, are fond of you and dearly love you as a friend, colleague, as a community of neighbors or as a church, and as family means they don't want to see you in such pain. Seeing you in pain is a source of pain for them in itself! This secondary type of grief can be distressing especially to family such as parents, siblings and in-laws. They do care, and sometimes you can be amazed at the level of care the wider community show through prayer or material and emotional help.

It is true they may not assume your personal responsibilities such as financial obligations and being there for those left behind. But indeed they care.

Receiving their comfort from this premise, makes it easier for you to process your raw emotion and tolerate their mistakes. Perhaps they say that coz it's the best they know how, they have never experienced it and are themselves distraught and afraid of distressing you further.

I think there is a healthy way of dealing with this and this is by choosing to receive the love and care that is coming from their heart. Their words may be flawed but their hearts are with you. So receive their hearts. That's the greatest gift they have brought to you.

Yes, people can improve, but perhaps this starts with you. Perhaps it starts with you understanding our mutual limitations. Perhaps it starts with you saying and doing the right things to others. If you are condoling others, perhaps simply saying something like this will help,

*'I am sorry,*

*'I can't imagine what your going through but please know I am praying for you'*

*'We celebrate our loved one for the life they lived, they were a blessing to us all'.*

## *God's comfort*

The other thing we can do is firstly allow ourselves to grieve as we discussed earlier. We need to allow ourselves to feel the raw emotion, tell God about it and then allow ourselves to receive God's comfort because he is the God of all comfort!

While man can only embrace us or comfort us with caring words.

God's comfort is internal. It comes from the premise that God is never overwhelmed with the tragedies of this life. We are not saying he is unconcerned, no but we are saying he is not overwhelmed.

God is in control in the midst of the flood. He remains enthroned as 'King of the universe'.

*The LORD sits enthroned over the flood; the LORD sits enthroned as king forever. Psalms 29:10 ESV*

God is also the 'Father of Spirits'. He knows that spirits don't die. He has placed and planted eternity within all of us! He knows that we are never really lost when we die.

When Job was tested he lost everything he had. He lost wealth and riches, he lost his 10 children too. When God restored Job he gave him double of what he lost of property and animals.

*"And Jehovah gave Job twice as much as he had before.*

*So Jehovah blessed the latter end of Job more than his beginning: and he had fourteen thousand sheep, and six thousand camels, and a thousand yoke of oxen, and a thousand she-asses. He had also seven sons and three daughters." Job 42:10, 12-13 ASV*

This can be compared to what he had in the beginning

*"There was a man in the land of Uz, whose name was Job; and that man was perfect and upright, and one that feared God, and turned away from evil. And there were born unto him seven sons and three daughters. His substance also was seven thousand sheep, and three thousand camels, and five hundred yoke of oxen, and five hundred she-asses, and a very great household; so that this man was the greatest of all the children of the east."*

*Job 1:1-3 ASV*

This comparison shows us that indeed he had double of everything..... but not quite... everything was doubled except the number of children. This tells us something because if God gave him double then he ought to have have doubled his children too.

But remember that God was doubling everything and not tripling them. If he had given him 20 more children (assuming his wife's body could handle it, unless with divine help) he would have got his mathematics wrong because 10 were already with him in heaven. The first set of children were never lost! They were and are in God's presence to this very day. For this reason God could not give him anything more than 'another ten children'.

Once you realize that our loved ones are never lost the narrative changes.

We don't talk about eternal life as an anesthetic to the fear of dying, not at all, we talk of life after death because it is true! Because God is true! Because his word is true and because heaven is real! The problem is we don't believe it. That's why this book is called 'transition' because we merely transition! We shift from one dimension to another, from one world to another, from the physical to spiritual!

It's real dear friend! It's real, once we realize this we will mourn but not despair, we will be pressed on every side but not crushed in spirit. You will be tried and tested but will not feel abandoned by God! When loss happens you might be startled, found dumb or dumbfounded, left speechless with nothing to say, confused, bewildered, stupefied and reeling as if a hammer has hit your head, stunned and trying to keep your balance. But at the end of it all you will not abandon hope or lose heart!

### *Other triggers of raw emotion*

There are so many triggers of pure and raw emotion that you can encounter along the journey of grief and we will explore some of them.

My triggers included church services, instead of being with my wife and kids, I was now alone with the kids. I thought going to church would be easy but boy was I wrong! I wet many tissues in the first month as tears streamed down my face in remembrance of my new state of loneliness.

This very thing happens to many people when they discover that they now have to sleep alone on their bed or sit alone on their couch for example. It could also be the lonely ride to work, or the lonely jog or weekend or early morning walk if you did these things together before.

Others have experienced very vivid dreams of the loved ones.

Dreams usually come from the abundance of thoughts and wishes for the return of our loved ones. People have experienced dreams in which the loved ones talk them, plan with them and even interact and touch them, only to realize that it was all a dream.

Before coming to reality they wonder how the doctor could have gotten the diagnosis wrong and how much a case of 'mistaken identity this funeral was'. Perhaps they would try to pinch themselves in the dream and see that nothing is happening and they are not waking up. Confident that they are not dreaming they start to feel significant relief. But as surely as the sun rises... all dreams surely come to an end and soon we are awake. We then blame our subconscious and ask how this could be? How could the mind be so cruel and inconsiderate of our emotions?

Sometimes other triggers include numerous challenges experienced during the funeral. In most of the world the funeral process may not be as smooth as should be. It could be affected by culture and some practices which may not be in line with your personal faith. There may also be some practices which can be emotionally taxing and at times physically harmful, all these require loving relations who can be, not only so kind but also, bold enough to protect and speak for the grieving family.

Sometimes people will want to take advantage of others by overpricing funeral services and simple greed and extortion in order to make a quick buck.

Other challenges could be limited resources or no family support during the funeral. This causes trauma because we wish we could do more but are not able to do so.

In 2020 most parts of the world were affected by the corona virus called Covid 19. This meant the burial services were not always normal or handled with dignity as per cultural or religious practices. The manner in which our loved ones can be handled in such situations may cause us pain. The politics around this matter could also be confusing with crooks seeing opportunities for making quick money as they play on the desperation of the bereaved. I have known some people to demand unreasonable sums of money accompanied with threats of not burying their loved ones until certain things are done or paid for. Such crimes must be reported to relevant authorities so they stop their folly.

Simple sight of your loved ones clothing can trigger pain. Clothes of your baby, child, brother, spouse or parents can remind you of the loss as you face the reality that these will never be worn again by them.

Simple perfumes, fragrances and scents inside the house and on clothes can be painful reminders of your loss. Sometimes you may meet someone who wears the cologne of your loved one. This too is painful! But over time we learn to accept the loss since we can't tell people to stop wearing their cologne.

Sometimes shots of pain are felt when we try to fill the gap left behind. The gap could be emotional, physical or financial. As you step in the gap, we are reminded of how important our loved ones where. We discover that the things we took for granted actually require a lot of effort and discipline. They are cherished even more in their absence as a result.

Mannerisms, including the funny, and silly things of our loved ones is what we sometimes remember most, if it's the older generation this mostly relates to things they never understood about us and we, about them. If it's spouses and partners it's probably something they never got around to master and always needed you to step in. They knew it always bugged you but were happy to see you give in to their small and sometimes silly requests. It could be something so small as they can never make their own tea, or fetch their own glass of water. You would always step in and help but you recall these things and say, 'why did he go, he would have been asking me for his glass of water by know?'

I talk of a glass of water because one interesting thing about my wife Debbie was that she always cherished a glass of water..... 'that was not served by herself'. We would serve both our meals, start chatting and eating and in the middle of a bite she would go silent. In amazement at her silence I would look over to her and wonder why the silence. My eyes would be met by her classic dog puppy eyes looking ever so sad... straight into mine! 'What's wrong sweetie? Is there something wrong with the food?' I would ask.

*'hey darling, do you know that water is tastier when it's served to you?'*

That would be my cue to get her a glass of water and I used to feel disturbed every time but one look into her eyes would win me over... all the time!

Yes, I would protest here and there and it would be a daily routine until I sometimes got the better of her and just gave her a glass of water before starting my meals. Sometimes she would appear in the middle of my meal and the routine would start.... and oh yes it would end the same way, with a little protest, but it would definitely end the same way! I am sure she was having fun!

So even if she is at the table with a jug of water within inches of her and I am further away, she would say the same line

*'hey darling, do you know that water is tastier when it's served to you?'*

*'Umadziwa kuti Madzi ogawilana amakoma?'*

No matter what I would be doing I would have to drop it and giver her the 'tasty' glass of water.

Over time as my protests grew wiser, I would say

*'honey, can you change your request slightly please?'*

*Can you please add 'honey please stop whatever you're doing' and then say 'and fetch me a glass of water?'*

She would laugh but won me over, with her puppy eyes, all the time! What I loved though, was that she would be over the moon whenever I serve her that glass of water and show her that she is important and is my priority. That would simply 'make her day', um er 'make her meal' rather.

It is such little things and mannerisms that can trigger fond memories of your loved ones.

Other things that can bring fond memories, pain or sorrow are things like family photographs and videos. Seeing them in still or motion picture and hearing their voices again in a video almost makes them alive and can be fond reminders of how precious they were to us.

One last thing I can consider is the new experience of writing and talking about our loved ones in the past tense. Anyone can do this but we are mostly sensitive to this when others do it and we remind ourselves that indeed that is how we ought to refer to them. There is a bit of resistance at first as we think that 'it should never be like that' but the sooner we acknowledge reality the better.

### *Being ever sensitive*

I believe that we are all tasked with being ever sensitive when we are around friends and family and others who have experienced loss in one way or the other. A friend of mine who is a widow once drove with a bubbly friend of hers. As they drove along the country side all her bubbly friend was talking about was 'my husband this' and 'my husband that',

'this is my husbands car, he bought it for me, he is very loving and caring, he is a man among men' and so on and so forth.

By the time they came back from the trip she was devastated and fell into a depression because as a widow she missed the good things her husband was doing, not out of choice but of tragedy. She told one of her close friends that she wants to quit serving on the committee of the youth ministry she was serving on because the talk of her friends was really destroying her. She was encouraged to continue serving and she did, but this only tells you how sensitive we should be when relating to those experiencing loss.

If they had lost a husband, let's take care about how we talk about our own husbands, if a wife, take care how you talk of your own wife, if a son, take care of how we talk about our own or if a daughter then how we talk of our own daughters. We are called to be ever sensitive and accommodative so they also feel embraced and supported.

Some spiritual folk naively condemn and say

*'you ought to have had more faith,*

*ought to have prayed more,*

*ought to have fasted not just prayer alone,*

*you should not have missed this anointed meeting and church service.*

To be honest this is stupidity of the highest order and we should not partake of, or perpetuate it. God is sovereign and in his wisdom and sovereignty he allows certain things to happen whether good or bad. Remember that we are called to be ever sensitive, ever caring and ever loving!

# 11

# How to receive God's comfort

Life is full of reminders of our loved ones and because of this there will be so many triggers of raw and painful emotion. As can be seen, these will be situational, social and personal. But what is common is that not all will be intentional or within our control. What is important therefore is to navigate them safely. We can do this by *deciding* to acknowledge that people have their limitations and choosing to see the good in them.

More importantly, however, is to receive God's comfort. This is superior to that of men because God is superior to man. This is also because God has a special role and ability to comfort his people. He is so very able that he has earned a name for what he does. He is called 'The God of all Comfort'. As we know names can describe the intentions and purpose and the ability of someone. And God's intentions and purpose are to comfort you and heal you. He has the ability or capabilities and the capacity to comfort you!

*'Blessed be the God and Father of our Lord Jesus Christ, the Father of mercies and God of all comfort, who comforts us in all our affliction, so that we*

*may be able to comfort those who are in any affliction, with the comfort with which we ourselves are comforted by God.' 2 Corinthians 1:3-4*

Man's comfort comes from outside in the sense that it is external to us while God's comfort starts and bubbles from within us! Therefore it is so much more effective and once we hold on to it we are able to navigate all the triggers of pain and raw emotion that we encounter on a daily and frequent basis. I think that embracing or receiving God's comfort is a key to your healing in life. And there are several things we need to do for us to experience this.

First of all, we have to believe in God. Jesus tells us that we should believe in God the father but also we should believe in him as the son of God.

But what are we to believe? I think we ought to believe what he told us in John 14.

*"Let not your hearts be troubled. Believe in God; believe also in me. In my Father's house are many rooms. If it were not so, would I have told you that I go to prepare a place for you? And if I go and prepare a place for you, I will come again and will take you to myself, that where I am you may be also." John 14:1-3*

Jesus told us about a God who has several attributes. Firstly, he was not talking of a dead God, he was rather talking of a living God. So first of all our God is alive! He is unlike idols that cannot talk or hear.

Secondly, he says we should believe not only in this living God but also in Jesus. Why is this so? Because Jesus is the representation of his father and both of them are true! We should also believe in Jesus because he is the physical representation of an invisible God. In Jesus we have physical evidence of the reality of this invisible God that we call Yahweh. Logical right? Yes it's logical and it's not only logical, it's thoughtful of God to do this.

*"Jesus saith unto him, Have I been so long time with you, and dost thou not know me, Philip? he that hath seen me hath seen the Father; how sayest thou, Show us the Father?*

*Believe me that I am in the Father, and the Father in me: or else believe me for the very works' sake."*

*John 14:9, 11 ASV*

Thirdly, he says we should believe about heaven! But what should we believe about heaven? I think the very mention of it means we should believe heaven is real!

We should also believe that heaven is not a grave! There is no cemetery in heaven neither are its inhabitants zombies! Why do I say this? Because heaven is alive! It is inhabited by a living God! And it's also inhabited by living people.

The problem with most of us is that we believe that a living God has dead children! Oh yes! And you might be one of them and I can show you why!

Do you have any close or distant relative that does not live in your neighborhood, town, city or state? And even those who live in another country whether on your continent or overseas? There is a good chance you do, but if you don't then do you have friends in that situation? If not then at least do you know someone who lives abroad?

I always wonder how we handle ourselves in these situations when a relation goes to a far away country or to a different state without ever coming back. Perhaps only coming back on special family events once in a long long while! Or when people migrate to distant lands in search of good fortunes but end up not communicating and even abandoning their family.

The emotions we feel can be loneliness and in some case abandonment. When you think about it do you wake up every day crying for your relations? Do you start sobbing for them because they are looking for better fortunes elsewhere? Do you give up living your own life because your brother is far away from you? If your parents are far away do you wake up crying for them everyday? No? Not at all right?

Yes you might say 'I talk to them often' but there are others with whom you don't talk daily or as regularly and sometimes you don't really talk at all! So why don't we wake up crying for them daily? The reasons may be several including the extent of our contact with them but most of all we know that 'they are alive! This is the single most important reason we don't mourn for those that are far away from us!

If people heard us wailing and mourning at the crack of dawn they would quickly rush to support and comfort us thinking something terrible has happened. And assuming you're in a very close knit culture that does not need an invitation to a funeral like most non western or non European cultures the whole neighborhood would gather around you. Imagine their surprise upon asking who has died and you say,

'no one has died, I just miss my sibling brother who left the country 10 years ago!'

Now the fact that they are far away does not mean we don't miss them. Of course we do. We wish they had shared a Christmas, Easter or Thanksgiving dinner with us. Or that braai or barbecue but we simply accept the facts and live our lives. We have peace that they are not only alive, but also that they have a better quality of life than us. We talk about them as being in a developed country. Perhaps with a sense of pride that one of our own is well exposed and in a better country than ours.

So, what changes in a funeral situation? The change is that we feel sorrowful because we know that they have died and are no longer alive. Even if we would never have talked with them again we now mourn their death because it is now certain and settled that indeed you will never meet them.

But is this true? I think not! It is as untrue for those who die in distant lands as it is for those who die in your proximity. They are not lost for ever! Why? Because God has planted eternity in their hearts!

There is something about living that gives us comfort and something about death that robs our confidence. The same distant relations are now mourned, our hearts are pricked and we feel deep sorrow as a result. The reason is simple they are dead. Or so we think!

But as indicated, God has planted within them his breath of life which is his eternal flame of life. That person exists but not in this dimension. When someone close to you, who was in your proximity and who you interacted with dies they too are not lost. Thy have simply gone to a distant land! Do you know that to believe this you must really believe God? Most people are hopeless because, if truth be told, *they don't really believe God!* They are like the disciples who were told that Jesus will rise again but could not really grasp the concept.

"He hath made everything beautiful in its time: ***also he has planted eternity in the heart of man.***" Ecclesiastes 3:11 ASV

Now, I submit to you that heaven is a real place, it is more real and more permanent than earth. And that heaven is inhabited by a real God, a living God and that this living God has living offspring that he brings back home in heaven. He is actually called the God of the living and not the dead! We have discussed this elsewhere that he is called the God of Abraham, Isaac and Jacob he is not a god of the dead but of the living!

Do you know that your loved ones who died here on earth are alive? Do you know that they simply relocated to heaven? That they merely transitioned? And went to another country?

The problem for us is how they transition? We fail to process how they transition. We see a dead body and think the spirit is trapped within that body and that the spirit is also dead! Imagine if there was a very special airline that flys us to heaven? We would receive the message that we are going to heaven on such such a day, we would announce to close family that please bid me farewell and take me to the airport. It would be a few tears but not despair.

We are also traumatized by the circumstances of our loved one's death. We look at how wasted their bodies have been, by disease, how bruised and battered by injury. What we forget is that we are looking at a piece of clothing that has been torn and the real person is still whole, even if they were disabled in life, their spirit is whole. We forget that we simply are looking at an envelope when the letter is in God's hands. We are looking at how the envelope has been opened... perhaps not with a letter opener to be as smart as possible, but with bare hands and a large tear, in such a messy manner!

Imagine if all of us were transported to heaven in a chariot of fire and a divine whirlwind. The obituaries section of our news papers would be called, 'transition announcements' or 'chariot visits' or 'chariot homecomings' they would be more celebratory than sombre, descriptively captivating as they emphasize and explain the glory of each chariot encounter, celebrating the glory and beauty of each chariot. Chariots befitting king's and nobles! But God has chosen that we use a human way, the envelope way, whereby the envelope is worn out and brutally torn and these tears are painful to watch and remember.

If we focus on the fact that God is alive and our loved ones are alive, and look beyond the envelope I think everything would change. I think we would know they are in a better place. That they are safe, that they are peaceful and that they lack nothing. And being in God's very presence they are probably in the best place that anyone can ever be!

But, what does it really mean to doubt that our loved ones are alive? I think it means that if they are dead then the one who gave them life has failed? Perhaps he himself is dead, because he has failed to sustain the life of his sons and daughters. To believe our loved ones are dead means that, at least, if God is not dead then his authority is not absolute. It would mean he is only God of the earth and not heaven! Because his authority is only limited to the planet earth where there is life! If God is a god of the earth alone, it also means God is a fraud! He is lying to us that he made the heavens and the earth, that heaven is his throne and earth his footstool. He cannot be god of one and not the other. He cannot be alive in one dimension and not the other. It means his reputation has and is, until now, riding on the creative power of another god who has authority in both domains because you cannot have the power to create and yet have no power to reign over your own creation. If our loved ones are not alive, it means God himself is dead! It means he has failed to sustain the spirits of our loved ones and Jesus is not the way the truth and the life after all. Just one falsehood from the mouth of God or one limitation in the ability of God means his whole integrity is flawed. It puts into question everything about him!

So we must know that God is true and we must believe that God is alive and that his children are also alive. To believe otherwise is illogical and perhaps it is truly madness as illustrated in the poem below *(with some five consecutive words in the first paragraph in the Chichewa language);*

*Me crazy, me ...*

*To believe God is true on some things and not others? And of earthly blessings and not heavens reality! Me crazy, me!*

*Me crazy, me, coz I don't wake up every day crying for my family and friends in distant lands, otchona, obeba otsogola anzathu akunja. (Overseas or countries with better fortunes)! Me crazy, me!*

*To know that even though I don't talk to them, they are safe where they are, they are alive where they are and have a better quality of life! They are happy where they are, even if they are not on Facebook and I can't see any of their videos or pictures. I am still happy for them and I celebrate them. Me crazy, me!*

*When I hear of their demise, oh the pain and sorrow I feel! I will mourn the gap left behind, the smiles, the jokes and the encouragement I no longer have. Oh the pain of the gap! Can I be me and be them all at once! Me wondering, me!*

*To think that earth is more real than heaven? Is God true and believable about earth's reality and not about heaven's reality? Me crazy, me!*

*Shall I only mourn those in the distant land of heaven and not those in distant lands on earth? Or shall I start this now? Me crazy, me!*

*To think that I am at ease coz they are alive on earth! Yet despair when they migrate to heaven? Me crazy, me!*

*Are they not alive in heaven? but only on earth? Me crazy, me!*

*To believe that God is...., not was, the God of Abraham, Isaac and Jacob, the God of the living and not the dead? Yet not believe that our loved ones are also alive? Me crazy, me!*

*To doubt the reality of heaven and still think that 'God is' 'God exists' Me crazy, me!*

*To think only God is real and his home is not? Me crazy, me!*

*That only God is real and alive and his offspring are not? Me crazy, me!*

*That heaven can be real and our loved ones not? Me crazy, me!*

*That earth is real and heaven is not? Me crazy, me!*

*To think that he is only God on earth and not beyond it? Me crazy, me!*

*Me crazy, me! So help me mourn the gap left behind,*
*Hold me God as I dread the task of being what I cannot,*
*Of wearing shoes I cannot,*

*To be a father and a mother all in one!*

*As I battle the emptiness, the loneliness, the silence and the craziness!*

*To celebrate the life that was lived on earth, and that is being lived in heaven!*

*Because me....*

*Me crazy, me!*

### *Choose to please God with faith and let not your heart be troubled*

I think, we need to make some choices about God. Firstly, we need to choose to believe him. Choose to take God at his word. We need to know that his care is real and then to put our trust in him.

The reality of God's care is seen throughout scripture. He translated Enoch and transmitted him to heaven. He took Elijah in a chariot of fire and a whirlwind, he raised Jesus from the dead, he raised many righteous people in Jerusalem from the dead on resurrection morning! He came and appeared to Steven when he was being stoned. He is simply the shepherd of our souls. He said

*'And if I go and prepare a place for you, I will come again and will take you to myself, that where I am you may be also' John 14:3*

We need to believe that we cannot be with Jesus and in the presence of a living God and be dead at the same time.

We also need to believe that if we have Jesus we have the keys to Heaven's Door. He is the way to Father. He is our shepherd and he is the door! Jesus is the answer and the key.

Jesus started with a conclusion when he said 'let not your heart be troubled'. This is 'the conclusion of the matter' and the only point he was trying to make.

He explained many things why we should not be troubled but the main point is.... our hearts should not be troubled. Why?

Because you have a father

Because your father has a house

In his house are many mansions!

Jesus is planning for your stay in heaven
Jesus is the architect of your mansion
Jesus is the builder of your house
Jesus is the interior designer of your mansion
Yes, he is actually preparing a place for you!

Jesus does not lie about heaven and if it were not true he would not have told us about heaven.

At our point of death Jesus is there with us.
Jesus will come to take us home!
Jesus is alive
God is alive
Our loved ones are alive
We will live in his presence
We will be where Jesus is!
So it's up to you to make a choice,
to believe God
to please him with faith and ultimately,
to 'not let your heart be troubled!'
To grieve but not despair
To miss the gap filled by our loved ones but
not to lose hope and rather
To trust in God for strength.

To remember them when we encounter the many triggers of emotion but
to hope in the loving care of our father.

It's our choice, to not let your heart be troubled! It's not a naturally easy choice, but you can make small choices every day!

# 12

# Helping children with loss

Transition is as difficult for children as it is for adults and perhaps more so. This is because they will mostly not have the ability to express themselves as well as adults and most of the time they rarely understand what is happening around them when their loved ones die.

This chapter is dedicated to discussing how to help children with their loss. I do not think I may have all the necessary tips and also realize that there are many experts in the subject whom I cannot claim to overrule. I can only share some of the most acceptable practices of how to help kids especially learning from my own recent experiences. Some in which I could have done better and others in which I could not do much about.

### *When to tell them*

When a death happens it's important to tell the children as soon as is practicable. Situations will differ with each occurrence of death such as sudden death or long illness but telling them in a reasonable amount of time reduces their sense of confusion as they see things happening in preparation for and or during the funeral. They are at least able to understand why things are happening the way they are.

### *How to tell them*

Telling children about death is very difficult for adults because we naturally want to protect their feelings. However the realization needs to be made that they will also need to understand it and also heal from its effects.

The key principle is to ensure that you speak in a way they can understand. I posed the question of how to tell my kids about their mom's passing to a medical psychiatric expert who helped me as I was getting trauma treatment, firstly she enquired the ages of my children, to which I answered 3 and 5 years for my girl and boy respectively.

Knowing they were relatively young she simply advised to talk to them in a words they can understand. However she emphasized the need to help them understand the permanence of death.

It is important to use clear and simple words to enable the understand. So using words like dead or die helps ensure clarity of what has happened. This is difficult but important. Grown up words and euphemisms like 'passed away' 'passed on' 'gone to sleep' or 'lost' don't help much and cause more confusion. Considering the ages of my children, I must admit I found this to be hard and all I could say was that mommy has gone to heaven.

This did not do them much good as they then kept asking when she will come. I then had to explain that when people go to heaven they don't come back. Again, this is depending on the age of children and on how much they can understand.

If possible, it is better to tell kids that you have something sad to tell them. And that their loved one has died. It is also good to build on somethings they already know especially in deaths of natural causes such as illness. You could then say, 'I have something sad to tell you, Grandpa has died. He has been sick for a long time and and because of that he has died'. At least I managed to use this approach to my children when my Dad died.

You are likely to get a lot of questions. Answer them as honestly as you can and if you don't have all the answers you can honestly tell them you don't know.

### *Describing death to them*

Death is an alien concept to children but it's something they can still understand. It is important to describe it in simple terms again and tell them simple things like when people die their bodies stop working. Sometimes when people get too old they are not very strong because their bodies have lived and worked for a very long time and sometimes they don't work very well. Sometimes they get sick and they die because of it.

Also telling them that when people are dead they can't talk, or move or walk. Others have suggested to calm them by saying they can feel no pain when they are dead. This may be particularly helpful if the person suffered for a while and it can help them know that they are no longer suffering.

### *Dealing with their confusion*

Death can cause a lot of confusion to children and in their attempt to find meaning, they ascribe the death to many things. One common behavior is to think they caused the death. They sometimes remember the naughty things they had done and think perhaps that's why someone died. In my son's case, he struggled to understand when mommy is coming back. He asked if mommy was running away from him and if it's because he was naughty. I said no it's not because of you. You are a very good boy and we all go to heaven when it's our time. I ended up telling him that his mom had died, mainly because he asked if mom had died not that I had the strength to tell him. He was actually teaching me how to explain the situation to him. I thought he was not ready to know this but apparently he heard that mommy had died and wanted certainty. I can only imagine the confusion he had before verifying with me. I had to painfully confirm this to him but lovingly assured him that it's ok because he is not alone.

The other confusion I saw was the confusion of faith versus reality. Faith deals with what we believe has happened to our loved ones in terms of where they are, now that they have died. Reality is about their absence in our lives and the gap we currently feel. Telling them that our loved ones are in heaven can mask the truth and pain of dying. I had to tell my son that when we die we go to heaven. When he learnt that mommy died he cried uncontrollably. I let him cry but comforted him. He then asked if he will die too when going to heaven and I said that we can't go to heaven without dying. He then said but I don't want to die daddy. I said it's ok because when we die Jesus is with us, and takes us to heaven. And that he should not be scared.

The truth of the matter is that young minds do not fully understand the concepts of spirit, soul and body. It takes time for them to understand. You can only help them, understand death through a process and not a one time explanation. I think you walk with them and help them as they grow. When my son Sean was six years old I had to explain things again and I took him to his Mom's grave to put flowers together and I told him we are going to mommy's grave. Mommy's grave is where we buried Mommy when she died.

## *During the funeral*

The funeral is a difficult time because of the many events that take place in a short space of time. Sometimes kids are unable to understand what is happening to them during this time especially if they have not been told clearly. I did not realize the confusion that Sean had until after the funeral. I was injured myself and for the most part did not have my kids for the first two days of my wife's demise. Burial was on the fourth day and I still struggled to tell them. I thought I would have time to tell them, but discovered both time and courage where not in abundant supply.

However, I was asked why there were so many people around and why they were crying and sad and I told him they came to show that they were sad that mommy has gone to heaven because they miss her and that when we are in heaven we don't come back.

I have included a special section of my experience at the end of this chapter and I have called it 'a toy car for Jesus'. Based on the principles we are discussing now you will be able to gauge where I did well and where I did not. You may learn on what can be done better in other scenarios depending on your unique circumstances. You will also be able to reconcile theory and practice and see how important a balance of empathy, knowledge and wisdom is when we are applying these principles. After all wisdom is the right application of knowledge, not prideful and hurtful application.

In general, I would recommend telling the children what they need to know depending on their age and to consider death as a journey for them and not a one time event. This means you can always build up on the journey in the best way possible even though you might not have been the 'excellent expert' and in most cases you learn on the job. On the job training means you can only do as well as you know how. So don't really beat yourself about it. The most important thing is how to build on your foundations as you walk this journey.

With this background, it may be possible to explain what the funeral will be like. Sometimes you may be able to explain that there will be a coffin and that your loved one will be inside there. However, I emphasize that there is no rule of thumb with these things and it's important to gauge the maturity of the child and his level of understanding. As indicated before, the child usually pushes his own limits and as a parent or guardian you are the best judge of how much to push the child.

Viewing the body is something that happens with adults in most cultures. The question of whether to allow a child to view the body is also a delicate one. The child himself and the parent or guardian are to make judgement calls on this one. The child's personality may come into play here and it's something that needs careful consideration.

I consciously decided not to let my two year old and five year old daughter and son view their mom's body. I recalled my own trauma when I viewed the body of my late grandma. I viewed the body when I was about 14 or 15 but the experience was traumatic to me and truth be told, I still have that image seared in my mind to this very day. Now it's a little faint, but it's still there. Strangely, I have gone to many viewings but this first viewing at a tender age, or not so tender, is the one that remains with me so strongly ever since. I once explained this to someone who let his children view their mother's body and he simply brushed me aside and almost casually said, 'it's because it was your first viewing'.

What ever you decide for them, do it in love and most of all sometimes we ought to remember that they are just kids and if telling them of everything else or involving them generally in the funeral is helpful, you may not need to push them too far.

If they are teenagers perhaps they could make a decision and even if they decide to view, they should be under no pressure and be reminded that they can change their mind at any point even at the last minute.

### *How children understand and deal with death.*

Children's ability to deal with death is largely dependent on their age and relative maturity. Therefore their ability differs from a toddler to a five year old, to a teenager and so on. We will look at each of these and see how we can manage them.

### *Babies and toddlers*

Babies and toddlers should not be discounted in the grieving process. Most people think thy are too young to realize what is going on but the reality is totally different. Babies have been given unique abilities to identify their mothers and fathers at a very young age. Most mothers are recognized using sound even before the baby is born. After birth, the senses of sight and smell augment the sense of hearing. Fathers are equally recognized before birth, especially if they talk regularly to the child even within the womb.

At the baby stage it is true that they will not be an awareness of what is happening around them but one thing is for sure.... they will sense that someone important is missing. They will likely experience a sense of abandonment and the result of this may be a sense of insecurity, continuous crying and perhaps a disturbance in sleep and feeding patterns.

An example of this is when my daughter who was three at the time she lost her mum had her own sense of abandonment. She couldn't talk much but one day when I asked how she slept our conversation went something like this,

*'Morning baby girl*

*Morning daddy*

*Did you sleep well?*

*Yes!*

*What did you dream about?*

*I dreamt that mommy is coming home!*

That response tore me apart. It made me realize that she just could not ask questions or understand everything her brother could. All she was sensing is that mommy is not here! And all she wanted was for her mommy to come home. Over time I repeated the message that mommy is not coming home but I know it could be a while before it really settles.

### *Toddlers to 5 year olds.*

toddlers to 5 year olds have their understanding slightly increased and they can start grasping the concept of death. They will increasingly become curious and ask for more information to help them come to terms with the death. I have had an experience with this as has already been discussed regarding the questions I was getting from my son.

At this stage they may struggle to understand the permanence of death and will keep asking when the loved ones will return until they slowly get the picture. They may also struggle with the concept of being dead if they are very young.

They may therefore be found to be searching and expecting them to return. Sometimes they may act it out in play and may talk of or pretend play that a pet is dead for example. It's all about how they are trying to process their feelings so they need to be understood and as time goes they get to understand things better.

The side effects of the loss may be tantrums and anger. These tantrums may be coupled by comparison to loved ones and you may be blatantly told you are a bad parent or guardian. You must just take it with grace and be the best you can be for them.

They may also experience regression in some areas such as such as poor school performance, bedwetting, loss of interest in play and disturbances in eating and sleeping routines.

Separation anxiety is something I personally experienced with my son. He was afraid to let me go out of his sight. On certain days he would not allow me to go to work and would cry uncontrollably thinking I won't return. Sometimes this would be in the morning but also at lunch time if I drop him off from school he would cling to me so much that he would delay my return to work. There is some need for balance between tough love and empathy and I would normally be torn between the two. It was not easy on me either sometimes I would be too sensitive, would really feel down as I imagined how he was feeling. But over time he improved. I also realized that he was quite the clever kid who would also take advantage of my softer side to manipulate me into staying home. Eventually we managed to get through this phase together.

One thing I picked up was that he thought perhaps 'mommy ran away from me because I am being naughty'. I had to explain to him that it was not his fault. This is common with most children and it's one of the things we should emphasize over and over again until they have a free spirit. Free of guilt and self condemnation.

### *Primary school age*

At this age the permanence of death is grasped much better. However, with more maturity comes more contemplation and speculation. With this speculation comes a lot of self blame and sense of guilt. In some cases there may be a fear of death and or other items that caused the death.

One common error is for the family to put pressure on the children to fill the gaps of their parents or guardian. So telling them that , 'you are now the man of the house' can be quite overwhelming for them. A certain man lost his wife who left him a 13 year old son. This child did not come out of his room often. When talked to, he would give very brief answers and immediately returned to his room. It was clear he was not handling his mother's death very well. When the father asked how he was feeling he said he is sorry that he caused mom's death and that mom ran away from him because he was not listening to her instructions all the time. His dad went into detail to explain why and how the death happened and that it had nothing to do with him. He then saw the great relief on his son's face and from then his behavior changed for the better and he was more interactive and engaged with the rest of the family.

### *Secondary school age*

At this age children are battling to understand themselves through adolescence. They may have pressures with striving for independence and trying to fit in with their peers. They want to stand on their own as they look forward to adulthood but may be thrown off balance into a sense of dependence by the loss of a loved one.

It is often difficult for them to fully express themselves. After considering that others of their age may never have experienced loss they are not well understood. They feel different and can even be sidelined and alienated by their friends.

This can lead to depression and withdrawal and a sense of apathy and loss of the meaning of life in general. This is a dangerous outcome because it can lead to risky behaviors while looking for that spark in life to bring some meaning to what is an otherwise meaningless life. I have seen a few teenagers who are embittered and angry against God for their loss and it is important to encourage them and counsel them according the truth of God's word that God has not abandoned them.

The other common response is a sense of immense responsibility. They may feel immediately grown up and feel responsible for caring for their siblings. This is an emotional burden that is by no means light. It is important for friends and relatives to come in and provide support where they can.

*The following is a special insert of how I interacted with my son on his mom's funeral.*

*A toy car for Jesus*

*The funeral service had just ended it was time to mourn Debbie at home. We were directed by the deacons to get into the hearse. Here I was with my 5 year old son who had just endured a long service that had his mother's picture in front of a casket. But what was this thing that shone and glittered in Gold before him? Why was his mum's picture in front of it and above all why was his mom's name being mentioned in every other sentence that the preacher made? Sean did not know that his mother had died in an accident. Sean did not know that this was his mother's funeral service. He spoke of death on a sporadic basis. But mostly in relation to insects that had died around the house. For example he knew that you can kill mosquitoes either with a spray or with your bare hands if you're up to it.*

*He had seen his dad do this several times and had seen the dead mosquito fall or be thrown to the ground. When he found a dead centipede or millipede he would ask, 'daddy is this dead' ? 'Yes Sean' I would say, and still do whenever he sees something similar. The biggest thing he has seen die is a lizard.*

*So here I was, thinking 'I would make him have a quantum leap from the death of insects to the death of a person and let alone his own mother!'*

*That was sheer madness... I thought. As I sat in the hearse I put Sean on my lap. Confused at the service he sat silently, .... thoughtfully. Something was going on but he could not figure it out. His mom's name was mentioned numerous times but she was nowhere to be seen herself.*

*As the casket was moved into the hearse he looked back intently... curiously... Then the question came....*

*'Daddy what's that box.... is it a present' I thought to myself what should I answer him? But I knew that when a kid asks 'if it's something..' then that's what they most likely think it is. So I answered*

*'Yes Sean, it is a present '*

*'Ok daddy'*

*Barely 2 minutes later Sean asked*

*'Daddy who is the present for?'*

*My head spinning. I knew what to answer, or so I thought...*

*'It's a present for Jesus'*

*'Ok daddy'*

*'But Daddy' he asked a few minutes later*

*'What's in the present?'*

*The questions were not relenting neither were thy getting any easier. Here is someone who only knew that insects die, how will I tell him that his mother is in the casket? How will he take it? I could not tell him that by all means!, As in my books that would be cruel. Or so I thought*

*'There is a big beautiful flower in the present Sean a beautiful red rose flower'*

*'Ok daddy'*

*'Daddy'*

*'Yes Sean'*

*'Does Jesus like toy cars?'*

*Being a 5 year old the best present for Jesus, he thought, was a toy car and I knew exactly what to say*

*'Yes of course Sean, Jesus just loves toy cars'*

*'Like the one in your office and the one you bought for me?'*

*'Absolutely Sean! Jesus loves toy cars'*

*'Ok Daddy, then we should buy him a toy car and put in the present'*

*Ok Sean we'll buy Jesus a toy car ok?'*

*'Ok daddy'*

*Each question came in about three to five minute intervals as he was carefully processing all my answers.*

*'Aah but Daddy'*

*'Yes Sean'*

*'But I thought Jesus is in heaven?'*

*'Yes Sean he is'*

*'So how will he get his present?'*

*I again had to pause…. as I gathered my self trying not to cry in his face*

*'Oh Sean, don't worry, we will keep the present in a special place and somewhere safe and Jesus will come and take his present ok?*

*'Yes Daddy, ok Daddy'*

*For some reason he did not ask anything again. For some reason he was satisfied that I would buy a toy car for Jesus and put it in the present.*

### *Keeping Jesus' present*

*The church service had ended and now we were at the cemetery. I had to prepare Sean for what he was about to see. I made sure he does not see his mother in the casket. After all,… he would have been too confused I thought.*

*I had to manage him during the burial of his mom. So what would I tell him?*

*'Sean David my son' I said in an ever so endearing tone.*

*'Yes Daddy'*

*'Now we want to put Jesus' present in a special place ok? That's where Jesus will come and find his present ok'*

*'Ok Daddy'. And he continued playing with my phone.*

*They lowered the casket and I said 'now they are putting the present in a special place.'*

*'Ok Daddy'*

*When it was lowered Sean wanted to make sure it's safe and said*

*'Daddy, daddy, I want to see the present'*

*I knew I needed to handle this well. If I don't he would cause a scene, he would be restless and if I do, it will be out of order as people will wonder what I was trying to do. So I chose to attend to Sean's curiosity and be out of order.*

*I took him to the grave's edge and he looked down to his mothers casket. After confirming that the 'present' was indeed 'safe' he turned back and went to our seat. As we did so, the burial team started throwing concrete and dirt on top of the casket.*

*Then I saw a frantic Sean!*

*'Daddy why are they making the present dirty? Jesus does not like dirty presents! Why daddy why? Tell them to stop daddy'*

*It's ok Sean don't worry they will cover it in paper and the dirt will not make it dirty ok?' That was not my best answer but I had to tell him something. Immediately, I handed him over to my aunt who then distracted him until the burial was completed.*

*But one last task was pending...., Sean and I had to put a wreath on Debbie's grave.*

*'Sean dear'*

*'Yes Daddy'*

*'We now need to put a flower so Jesus can know that this is where his present is ok? Will you help me put the flowers there?*

*'Yes Daddy I will help you'*

*'Thanks so much Sean you're such a darling and your my good boy ok?'*

*'Yes Daddy'*

*Shortly I was called to lay a wreath on Debbie's grave. All the time writhing in the bodily pain of the road accident which had claimed the life of Debbie, Sean's Mum and my dear wife. I stood up again and said 'Sean let's go and put the flower'*

*Sean obliged and followed me. I held the wreath and allowed him to hold it with me and together we laid it down on Debbie's grave.*

*We then came together and sat down. My head spinning and wondering if I should have done better by Sean. But with each passing day and hour the decision to tell of his mother's demise, how she died and how to tell him lingered in my mind and I needed to get more guidance on how to break the news to him. At least his mother was laid to rest and at least he partook of the proceedings. I guess he will understand in time!*

*Where is mommy?*

*So it was the first day of school after the funeral of his mom. He had been away from school for two weeks now. He was in holiday mood and wanted to spend as much time away from school as possible. But his grandma was around to help him get ready for school that morning. She is such a sweet and gentle soul. That's where Debbie got her kindness from. She coaxed him from bed and prepared him for school.*

*Afterwards she coaxed him to have breakfast as I excited him about school and guitar lessons. But as surely as the sun rises the question of mommy came up as it was supposed to. Remarkably he had not asked too much about his mom during the funeral.*

*The day she died he asked that mommy should not go with me. But we all knew Sean. He can be quite the actor. He can play on your emotions and convince you to do something you did not anticipate. So we needed to be the adults on this one.*

*He said*

*'Mommy are you going to leave me alone?'*

*'No sweetie you're going to be with aunt Glady's' (Aunt Gladys was his nanny).*

*'You should come back mommy'*

*'Just go and drop daddy and then come back okay?'*

*'When Daddy finishes we can go and get him ok?'*

*Don't worry Sean I will go and when I come back I will make you hot chocolate'*

*You will make me hot chocolate?'*

*'Yes Sean … nice and yummy hot chocolate'*

*'Ok mommy'*

*As we left the house we laughed at Sean's logic and wondered how he easily accepted to let us go.*

*'It's the hot chocolate' Debbie said 'he loves hot chocolate'.*

*Then we laughed at his logic of dropping me first and then picking me up later in the evening. Our destination was to a church crusade there in a place that was 110 km away. There was no way we would make two return trips.*

*'Kids are something else' we both said as we left and thought through his flawed logic. So from the time his mom died that evening to the day of the burial the following Wednesday he really did not ask much about his mom. All he knew was that she will come and make him hot chocolate. But two weeks later*

*he still could not see his mom and this morning he stormed into my bedroom and demanded the truth from me.*

*'Daddy where is mommy?'*

*I looked at him and smiled... painfully so.... sensing the frustration and sense of authority from his voice I knew he had me in a corner.*

*'Mommy is not around Sean she has gone away'*

*'Has she run away from me?'*

*'No Sean it's not because of you'*

*By this time I took him in my arms and put him on my lap making sure he faces away from me while his back lay on my chest.*

*Tears streaming my cheeks I could hardly speak...*

*'Mommy is in heaven Sean, she is with Jesus!'*

*I forced out each and everyone of these words amidst a sob. Wiping my face in the process*

*'When is she coming back?'*

*This question tore my heart*

*'She is not coming back Sean. When people go to heaven they stay with Jesus and heaven is beautiful ok?'*

*'Yes Daddy' .....*

*'Are there bad people in heaven?'*

*'No Sean there are only good people in heaven and there is Jesus in heaven'*

*'With angels?'*

*'Yes Sean, with strong and beautiful angels'*

*'The angels have swords?'*

*'Yes Sean strong angels with big and strong swords'*

*'The angels chase the bad people?'*

*'Yes Sean they angels make sure there are no bad people in heaven, they chase them with their swords'*

*'Ok Daddy' he looked at my face and saw my eyes streaming with tears. I wiped them dry and he went to take his guitar. Though he could not play well, if at all, he strummed something as if to comfort me and lullaby me to some sense of calmness.*

*Oh the thoughtfulness! The kindness and compassion he had for me. It amazed me and made we want to cry some more but then I let him strum his little melody and he watched me as he tried to distract me from my sorrow with a series of questions. 'He stopped asking about his mommy and put me in a guitar class.*

*'What's this Daddy'*

*'The shoulders of the guitar? I asked*

*'Well done Daddy it's the shoulders'*

*'And what's this'*

*'The body of the guitar?'*

*'Yes Daddy ...And what's this?'*

*'The neck of the guitar!'*

*'Yes Daddy'*

*He asked me something which I got wrong but he politely corrected me and said*

*'this is also the body of the guitar Daddy'*

*Noticing I was calmer he then was at ease and left me to go and finish his breakfast.*

*'What had just happened?' I thought....*

*I had just been comforted by a 5 year old. But in this whole experience I broke down.*

*I cried my heart out for quite a while before I could leave my bedroom. It rekindled memories and reminded me of the permanence of my loss and the reality of the task before me to take care of these kids. A few minutes and a few very wet hankies later I calmed down and took the kids to school not just in an average way but with credit.... in other words 'on time' !*

*End of insert*

*Lessons learnt*

Looking back at my experience with Sean I can't score myself a hundred percent. I had never experienced something like this and I was so emotional myself. However with the wisdom I have gained in time, I saw that my shortfalls are not a lost cause. Where I was not able to clearly explain to Sean what had happened I managed to make up in time. And I still do whenever I find the opportunity. I failed to do better, at the time, because I myself was injured and was in hospital for a day. On being told of my wife's demise, the children were not in my care. I thought I would tell them but I failed to do so as my emotional state was also beaten and battered. I later thought I would do this in preparation for the church service but I flew straight to the funeral and arrived with no time to tell them anything hence my improvisation personal confusion.

However, I managed to later explain that mommy had indeed died. And I even took him and his sister Aretha at 3 and 5 years old to what I told them is 'mommy's' grave. As time went by I was able to share the truth with them in love and little doses so as not to overwhelm them. They taught me what they could handle and I gave them information according to their levels of understanding.

I also ensured that the video of the funeral ceremony is well recorded so that I watch it with him and explain fully that the present for Jesus is actually mommy going to heaven. These are my small efforts to be both honest, loving and encouraging to my children. I pray that with God's grace they will fully understand, and above all as they grow and read this book they will grieve with hope beyond this life and that they will heal by God's divine grace.

Though I did not let them view their mother's body, they will have an opportunity to watch the videos and currently they fully understand that mommy is not coming back.

Let me say that if you are a parent you know your children best in how to lovingly guard them and guide them in the truth especially with the knowledge of some of the important guidelines discussed in this book and many others like it.

So don't beat yourself up if you have not handled your children like an expert. There is no rule book to these things. All you can do is be truthful, be loving and be encouraging. I pray that God will give you the wisdom to minister to young children who have experienced loss. And that God will use you to bring healing to many!

# 13

# Transition minded

Transition is a certainty of life and because it is a certainty, wholesome reflection of it teaches us great lessons if we are wise. What we realize is that life is brief and finite and because of this, life is to be lived with a mindset that speaks to the certainty of transition. David spoke of this when he said,

*"Teach us to number our days, that we may gain a heart of wisdom." Psalms 90:12 NIV*

David compared the immortality of God and the mortality of man. The fact that God is from everlasting to everlasting and that man's life is like a fleeting shadow. And because of it, he says man ought to live wisely! (Psalm 90)

The wisdom for living wisely and living well is in acknowledging the brevity of life, the fact that it is so limited. He says we live up to 70 or 80 years and no more. Nowadays with modern medicine and care we may live longer but the point remains… it's limited and it's finite! Once you acknowledge this fact, something emerges within us! A heart of wisdom! This is what I am calling the 'transition mindset!' And being 'transition minded'.

*"" Lord, remind me how brief my time on earth will be. Remind me that my*

*days are numbered— how fleeting my life is. You have made my life no longer than the width of my hand. My entire lifetime is just a moment to you; at best, each of us is but a breath." Psalms 39:4-5 NLT*

A transition mindset asks to be reminded all the time of the brevity of life. The brevity of our lives is likened to a vapor and a mere handbreadth before a God who sees a 1000 years as one day!

*"A wise person thinks a lot about death, while a fool thinks only about having a good time." Ecclesiastes 7:4 NLT*

It is wise to think a lot about death because if we do so we will live wisely.

### *Eternity in our hearts*

The Bible says God has placed eternity in our hearts.

*"Yet God has made everything beautiful for its own time. He has planted eternity in the human heart, but even so, people cannot see the whole scope of God's work from beginning to end."*

*Ecclesiastes 3:11 NLT*

In the context of this scripture, a transition mindset is a mindset that knows that life is to be lived 'for the next' and that 'the now' is intertwined with 'the next'.

People who live with this knowledge know that they are greater than what others think they are, and life is greater than what they think it is! They know that life is bigger than themselves and than everything they think they are. It also means that what we do in this life affects the next life, it means that while this earthly life is temporal and limited, hidden within us is something so precious and so eternal! Within us is the Spirit of God, the breath of life, something indestructible.

A transition mindset therefore 'lives for eternity not just for now'. You must therefore learn about 'eternal ripple effects' and live for the next life today!

So, living for eternity is not about never dying on this earth or preserving your body in the hope of a scientific resurrection, or never leaving earth, no it's about living powerfully, living with impact, living to inspire others, serving your generation and doing things not for yourself but for posterity , what if this mindset where in governments or politicians? What investments would they make and how frugal would they be?

Eternity in our hearts also talks of the judgement of God. We must know that God is a righteous judge and that all our works will have a reward.

### *Living dependent on God*

Living dependent on God, means fully relying on him and also knowing that you are given the permission to be alive. It's both saying 'Lord help me' and 'thank you that you have allowed me to live'. It's a shift from 'self dependence', to 'God dependence' and from independence to reliance.

With this mindset we learn to commit our plans to God. Committing our plans to God means realizing that only he can bring them to pass if he enables us and enlivens us. The Biblical story of the rich man comes to mind whereby he made grand plans with his harvest and said to himself 'I will make merry and build barns'. But God said 'you fool this very night I will require life.'

In fact Paul puts it very well in Acts 17:28 '*and says in him we live and move and have our being*'. It means he gave us breath and that we are doing all we do because of this breath and if he is to take it back then we are nothing and remain lifeless.

*'When you hide your face, they are dismayed;*
*when you take away their breath, they die*
*and return to their dust.' Psalms 104:29 ESV*
*'If he should set his heart to it*
*and gather to himself his spirit and his breath,*
*all flesh would perish together,*
*and man would return to dust.' Job 34:14-15*

This all means that nothing is guaranteed and that whether or not you acknowledge or fear God, your life is in God's hands! If it's in God's hands then you must acknowledge that your plans can only succeed if he allows them.

*Come now, you who say, "Today or tomorrow we will go into such and such a town and spend a year there and trade and make a profit"— yet you do not know what tomorrow will bring. What is your life? For you are a mist that appears for a little time and then vanishes. Instead you ought to say, "If the Lord wills, we will live and do this or that." As it is, you boast in your arrogance. All such boasting is evil. So whoever knows the right thing to do and fails to do it, for him it is sin. James 4:13-17*

There are several things we are warned about and lessons we get from this passage

*Don't boast about tomorrow's whereabouts*

*Don't boast about tomorrow's fortunes and certainty of the gains you plan to make!*

*You don't control your outcomes, God does!*

*Your life is too short, as a vapor that appears and disappears instantly*

*You should commit your plans to God*

*If God wills he will answer your prayer*

*He will give you life*

*And he will give you good fortune!*

*Honor him in your planning*

*Acknowledge your reliance on him*

*Confess your reliance on him and say 'if the Lord wills, we will'*

*Acknowledge you are alive by God because;*

*The passage says if 'God wills we will live' I find that quite astounding and humbling*

*Acknowledge that you will and can only achieve, if the Lord wills! ("If the Lord wills, we will live and do this or that.")*

*Remember that you can only achieve with God's permission and enablement*

*Failure to trust God in your plans of tomorrow means you are in-dependent, not dependent, not reliant on, and self dependent of God.*

*Self reliance is a sin, it is idol worship in which 'you' are your own god and idol*

*Self reliance is therefore defined and revealed as 'evil' not just as a simple sin or a transgression, it is seriously evil!*

*You might not have known this, but now you know!*

*Now that you know, don't deliberately sin*

*If you continue to be independent and non reliant on God, you commit two sins; the sin of independence as you did in the past and the sin of disobeying the call to now become dependent on him, especially now that you know better!*

If you missed all this just remember one golden rule

*'Don't boast about tomorrow!'*

That's the bottom line!

## *Living in haste*

Knowing that you have limited time on earth means you have to live in haste! It means never to assume you will have all the time in the world and to live in a manner that will ensure you achieve the most you can in this short life!

The analogy that fits this aspect of haste is the feast of the Passover. It finds its origins in the land of Egypt when God commands Israel to sprinkle the blood of lambs on their door posts. Once they do this the angel of death passes their homes and their first born children are spared from the plague of death. But not so for the Egyptians. What's important here is the attitude they were to have when eating the Passover meal!

*""These are your instructions for eating this meal: Be fully dressed, wear your sandals, and carry your walking stick in your hand. Eat the meal with urgency, for this is the Lord's Passover."*

*Exodus 12:11 NLT*

*"And thus shall ye eat it; with your loins girded, your shoes on your feet, and your staff in your hand; and ye shall eat it in haste: it is the Lord's passover." Exodus 12:11 KJV*

Israel was told to eat in haste! With girded loins, shoes on their feet and their staffs in their hand! (Exo 12:11). They received this command because God was preparing them for their journey to the promised land. God wanted them to eat in a militant manner as the sojourners they were to become. Girded loins point to being ready for work and the journey, feet shod with shoes means being ready to walk and to proclaim the words of their faith in their God. Paul in his letter to the Ephesians also talks of the shoes of the gospel of peace and being girded with the belt of truth! As sojourners we are also to take the staff which is used for sojourning in the great outdoors. A staff is the tool that Jacob used and is mentioned on meeting his twin brother and returning to his father's land. Jacob recounts his sojourning to his brother Esau and says *'with my staff I crossed this Jordan'* and with this staff I came back (Gen 32:10). So the staff is a walking stick that is used on a long journey. I believe this is a type of and representation of the word of God. Which we need as a guide in this life!

So what are we saying? In this life you must know that you are not home! You are in a type of Egypt and your real home is heaven. That's why Paul said we look forward to a city whose builder and architect is God himself!

So we will not be here permanently, we are just passing through. We therefore need to know that the time we shall leave this earth we shall leave it in haste. Once the angel of death killed Egypt's first born Pharaoh immediately ordered the Israelites to leave. The good news is that God had already prepared them to leave in haste!

If we will 'leave' this life in haste, then we should 'live it' in haste too. Because when the call to leave this earth comes we won't have time for farming, for businesses, for work, for socializing or any normal human activities. The time to leave is the time to leave! So if you are doing something and working on something don't unnecessarily delay it, don't procrastinate and fail to start something, you must be quick, you must deliver, and you must see the outcome of what you do. Don't start things you never intend to finish, don't start things that are unreasonably beyond your resources. You are better off starting things you can finish and gradually build on those things to achieve something grander! Be wise, and choose which battles to fight, be wise and choose which cities and projects to build lest if you fail people will say look at him, he started something he could not finish.

*""But don't begin until you count the cost. For who would begin construction of a building without first calculating the cost to see if there is enough money to finish it? Otherwise, you might complete only the foundation before running out of money, and then everyone would laugh at you. They would say, 'There's the person who started that building and couldn't afford to finish it!' "Or what king would go to war against another king without first sitting down with his counselors to discuss whether his army of 10,000 could defeat the 20,000 soldiers marching against him? And if he can't, he will send a delegation to discuss terms of peace while the enemy is still far away." Luke 14:28-32 NLT*

## *Working while it is day*

Knowing that you have limited time helps you do important work while you have the chance. Your chance to do something is your lease of life! Therefore we need to use our time wisely because we don't know when we will be called home! This was echoed by Jesus when he said

*"We must quickly carry out the tasks assigned us by the one who sent us. The night is coming, and then no one can work."*

*John 9:4 NLT*

*As long as it is day, we must do the works of him who sent me. Night is coming, when no one can work. John 9:4 NIV*

We must first of all know that according to Scripture there are things that God planned for us to do and achieve on this earth that were prepared by him long before we were born.

*"For we are God's masterpiece. He has created us anew in Christ Jesus, so we can do the good things he planned for us long ago." Ephesians 2:10 NLT*

We should also realize that we are partners with God just as Paul says

*"We are coworkers with God." 1 Corinthians 3:9 TPT*

Once we realize that we have a purpose and this purpose is God's purpose, and that we are his coworkers and partners that he uses to establish his purpose we realize that our coworker is actually keen for us to do the task and in fact is highly reliant on us doing it. It's like two drivers in a rally race, one driver is the navigator while the other is behind the wheel! God is our navigator! He has the map in his hands and tells us which turns to take so we don't get lost and can reach the finish line! As a co driver he reads his map or pace notes which for us is the Bible and gives guidance through prayer and obedience, and by his grace in true co-driver fashion he warns us what lies ahead, where to turn, how hard the turn should be, either a hard right or a hard left, or a soft turn and so on! He tells us what obstacles to look out for and if we have problems on our journey he will provide the much needed car maintenance we want.

Once God tells what we ought to do we must hearken to the words of Jesus and say *'I must do the work of the one who sent me, the one who is with me as my co driver, I must do the work of my God who depends on me to establish his plans on this earth! And I must do it quickly!'*

So we must quickly and in much haste start and finish the work of him who has sent us on this earth. This we must do while it is day! While we have life because when night comes, no one can work. When night comes our chance is gone. You can no longer finish your dreams, you can no longer work, you can not do anything at all when your night time has come. All that remains is to lay down in the sleep of death. So my dear friend, be transition minded. Know that you are not here on earth for ever. That your co-driver is your coworker, that your coworker is God, and he has the blueprint for your life, he knows the things that were prepared for you long long ago! So do them with haste! You only have one chance and one shot at life. Die empty, don't leave anything for the next life, if you must struggle then struggle, if you must fail then fail, it's better to fail or die trying than to never have tried at all!

In fact if you don't do anything of importance it's an insult to those who have gone before you! They would have done more perhaps with half the life you have lived and the many opportunities you have squandered could have let them literally change the world! We are sitting on opportunities that others would have fully utilized and if they had a choice they would come back and finish those tasks but they can't! So my friend, don't insult those who are better than us, those who were more industrious, those who started but never had the chance to finish, those who already did more with less and were only looking for another opportunity similar to the one you are wasting! Don't insult them because we are no more wiser or more intelligent than them, we only have a lease of live that has not run to its end! Don't waste your lease of life. Do stuff! Don't sit idle!

When God asks you what you did with your life what will you tell him on judgement day! When he tells you that others did more with half the life and half the resources he gave you, what will you say?

Being alive today is not being more intelligent than those who died, or being more prayerful or more spiritual than those who died... no! being alive is simply grace! My friend.... Don't waste this grace! Don't waste this gift! Do stuff! And do it hastily!

### *No regrets*

A transition mindset helps you live a life of no regrets! This is a concept that many people around the world have shared their thoughts on! It is a deep philosophical question which many seek to answer. I may not have the luxury to discuss all that this topic entails but I think I can summarize it's most important truths!

I would summarize this by saying a life of no regrets is a life in which you say 'I did my very best'. It's not one in which you say I should have done better!

As the saying goes

*"The saddest summary of life contains three descriptions: could have, might have, and should have." ~ Unknown*

This saying holds true to most people who have lived an unfulfilled life. But it must not be so for us. Sometimes I ask myself how I can avoid this sense of regret. I sometimes look past at some of my key decisions made in respect of my career, faith, friendships, family, relationships and marriage. Sometimes I ask myself if I could have done better, in some cases yes and in some cases no. I find that in cases where I could not have done better, I would have made the same decisions, fallen in love the same way, married the same person, and chosen the same career and perhaps would have made the same turns or baffling decisions along the way. I discovered that, the decisions I made were not made to please people and neither would that serve as a factor again! I discovered that a majority of the good decisions I made were made in good faith! And with the best of intentions. I also saw that I made decisions with best available knowledge and information at the time. In a similar situation I would in most cases make the very same decisions. With hindsight of course there are always things you could have done better, but with human limitations we should always strive to do our best! in cases where I could have done better I might have sought more advise, more mentorship or reached to others more.

There are many things one can do to avoid a life of regret but these are some of the key principles as discussed. The following are a few more general ones.

### *Running your race*

Paul talks of running your race and says

*"I have fought a good fight, I have finished my course, I have kept the faith:" 2 Timothy 4:7 KJV*

The first thing to know is that you have *your* race! Your race is not my race, your purpose is not my purpose, your path is not my path! We all have our own race and we must run it. We must not compare ourselves with others, or envy others in their success. We must be inspired by them, yes, but we surely must not be enslaved by a feeling of inferiority! We must take pride in what we do!

Secondly Paul is simply saying,

*"I could not have done it better, I have done my part, I have done my best, I have given it my all."*

Can we say this? Can we seek to do our very best in all things. Can we say I couldn't have done better! Can you say I had my course and I have finished it! My job is done? That's what "no regrets" means, that's why you must do what you need to do on this earth while you have the chance!

This is what fighting the good fight really means! I think this is a deep thing, a fight is about striving to do better, fighting injustice, and even defending the weak. A fight comes at a cost. You cannot fight and not put your infantry at risk. You will lose some men. But at the end of the day you must fight for that which is worth fighting for! You must not avoid good fights, even if they are long battles, you must be true to your feelings of the injustices you see and you must be true and not conform to those around you who see no wrong in injustice or who perpetrate them. You must fight discrimination, you must fight xenophobia, you must fight tribalism and you must fight racism, you must fight nepotism, and you must fight deliberate and systemic oppression. These are not easy battles but they are noble and sacred. So fight the good fight!

Thirdly you must keep the faith! Can you say you have been true to your values? Can you say you held on to what you deeply believed in? Can you say you cling to your faith? Were you a man of faith in all seasons? Where you holding dear to your values when all was well or were these values discarded as not convenient when times changed and were tough?

You must have raw integrity, raw allegiance to your God, uncompromising and unflinching commitment to your values and your faith. That's what keeping the faith means! Paul was imprisoned for his faith, he was beaten and tortured for his faith and endured many trials because of it. But through them all he was able to say 'I have kept the faith!'

My heart's cry, therefore, is that you too may say so!

### *Serving your generation*

We have extensively discussed the issue of running your race. But one man ran his race in such a way that he was uniquely described and appreciated by God. He did not make this judgement himself. Paul speaks of this and says

*"For David, after he had served his own generation by the will of God, fell on sleep, and was laid unto his fathers, and saw corruption:" Acts 13:36 KJV*

*For David, after he had served the purpose of God in his own generation, fell asleep and was laid with his fathers and saw corruption, Acts 13:36 ASV*

This verse encapsulates what we are discussing but summarizes it in a unique way. First, it talks of the purposes and will of God! We all have to serve and live by the will of God! These are purposes prepared before hand that we should walk in. Then we see David himself as an instrument that God is using to be a blessing. Then we see his generation! In this verse we see the three dimensions in which we ought to live in this world. The first is God, the second is the individual and the third is others! This is how life works or ought to work! If you receive such a verdict by God you will have done well!

Your life is not yours alone it is meant to be a blessing! Not only a blessing for self enjoyment but for the betterment and improvement of the world around you, the people around you, your family, your friends, your community and your nation. But not just your nation but also the whole world at large.

It is extreme wisdom to serve both God and man before we sleep the sleep of death. If we sleep having only served ourselves we have lived a tragedy! We will die in silence with no one to say,

*"I have been blessed by him that sleeps here".*

Tis a moral calamity to sleep without blessing your world! When you die the world must literally be indebted to you. It must consider itself to be in your your debt for the blessing of service you have bestowed on it! When you die you must have fought for a cause, you must have given yourself to the world, you must have pointed men to God and to the importance of and certainty of his eternal kingdom, a kingdom that outlives the ones on earth!

Like Paul, you must describe yourself as a 'drink offering' that is being poured out to the earth. You must know that you are not your own.

You belong to the purposes of God and remain bound to serving the earth in which God has placed you!

*"For I am already being poured out like a drink offering, and the time for my departure is near." 2 Timothy 4:6 NIV*

*"As for me, my life has already been poured out as an offering to God. The time of my death is near." 2 Timothy 4:6 NLT*

*"And now the time is fast approaching for my release from this life and I am ready to be offered as a sacrifice."*

*2 Timothy 4:6 TPT*

The translations above render interesting meanings they all speak of an offering. The NIV says the present life is being poured out as an offering. That's how we should live our lives as we serve beyond ourselves! We should pour ourselves into the lives of others.

The NLT renders it differently, it says my life is already committed. It is already given and set apart for a purpose. It's already set in the heavens that I will serve God, it's already settled that I will serve mankind. It has already been given and surrendered. Just as Samuel was dedicated to serve in the temple by Hanna, so is our life dedicated to God. Just as Samson was set apart from birth to be a Nazarite, to drink no wine and to never cut his hair for the deliverance of Israel so have you been set apart and committed and given to God as an an offering. Just as John the Baptist was set apart from birth to be a forerunner of Jesus, preaching and announcing the coming of the kingdom of God, preaching repentance from sin living a life of seclusion in the desert. With fearsome warnings of God's judgement, so also have you been set apart.

All these were drink offerings to their generations, all these had their lives poured out and all these had their lives fully engaged and fully committed. It was settled in heaven and it was settled on earth and it was settled in their hearts that they are to serve their generation!

The passion translation, TPT, gives an interesting rendering and says there is a sacrifice but it's a sacrifice of dying for the purposes of God! In other words he says I am ready to die and for my life to be offered in death as a sacrifice. That is a totally different meaning. While most of us run from death he is offering himself as a living sacrifice that is ready to die. He is literally putting his life on the line! He knows there is persecution ahead of him, he knows he will die but he says his death is not just a martyrdom! No, martyrdom is partly about God and partly about man. When we suffer for Christ we have some personal encouragement, and perhaps some personal glory that 'I have been honored to die as a martyr,'.

The book of Acts gives us a glimpse of this personal glory when it says

*"The apostles left there rejoicing, thrilled that God had considered them worthy to suffer disgrace for the name of Jesus." Acts 5:41 TPT*

Paul however has a different feeling, it's a feeling of humility and a feeling of surrender. It's the feeling that Hanna had when she gave up Samuel. It's the feeling of loss, and losing control, knowing that you want to raise and keep your own child but you have to give him up to God. It's a painful feeling of being torn apart, not by someone else but yourself! It's a feeling of pulling yourself limb from limb a putting the, on the alter as a living sacrifice and it's painful!

At this point you choose to be like Jesus, to lay down your life! To know that you can live but you now have to die. This is a battle that Paul had. At one point he almost had a choice! He said I would rather be with God but for your sakes I will be with you for your edification! With so much anointing and grace on his life there was a time he could talk to God and God would hear him. God would give him a lease of life to continue ministering, just like King Hezekiah he was given a new lease of life! But the time came when he had ran his course, he had fought the good fight, and he had kept the faith. At this point he needed to yield in sacrifice, he needed to yield to the sacrifice of death and the finality of this life! He probably might have been afraid in a human sense. He knew that heaven lay before him and he needed to be released from this life! He needed to experience death just like anyone else. Like most of the apostles he was imprisoned. Paul heard the stories of how the rest of the apostles died and it must have brought fear in him!

He heard that Peter was crucified upside down! Andrew was crucified and tied to a cross in an X shape, James was put to death by the sword, Thomas was put to death by stabbing him with spears and other stories of the apostles' death.

He knew he would suffer a similar fate and made peace with the fact that he too was a sacrifice and his death would be a sacrifice. Death is not always pleasant and how we die is not in our control. Sometimes knowing this means that you are afraid of death. Like Paul, we too hear stories of how people have died, and the pain, the suffering and the pangs of death that engulf them in their final moments. But, instead of being afraid, look at your death as a release from this life and also as a sacrifice!

Serve your generation to such an extent that even if you are imprisoned, victimized and stigmatized, even if you are castigated and eliminated by seclusion and death you are comfortable you are serving God and that even your death is a sacrifice.

It also means sometimes God does not answer our prayer for a new lease of life. Unlike Hezekiah, God may not give us 15 more years and if by his grace we were once spared then at the end of this new lease, death still has to be faced! Hezekiah had to yield to God's will when his 15 years were up. He died in obedience to God's plans and God's will. He yielded and accepted that he be taken to rest with his father's!

So remember, your life is an offering that was set apart long ago! Your life is currently being poured out and even your death is a sacrifice to God!

That is the most effective way to live and serve your generation!

May God help you to be sold out to him and his purposes! May God help you to serve your generation!

### *Be sure to live your purpose*

So far we have seen how utterly important it is for us to serve God and walk with him as our co driver and also about serving your generation. This is all about living your purpose. I just want to emphasize yet again the importance of this from a different perspective. What we must know is that purpose has the power to preserve your life and even to extend your life! This is what Paul experienced, firstly he almost had a choice of whether or not to stay on this earth, this choice and privilege was there simply because his purpose was not yet fulfilled. Only when his ministry was done and he was now in prison, was he ready to die without an opportunity for further extension or further privilege of choice.

We also see this in the lives of two other New Testament people. First we see Simeon in this passage

*"Now there was a man in Jerusalem called Simeon, who was righteous and devout. He was waiting for the consolation of Israel, and the Holy Spirit was on him. It had been revealed to him by the Holy Spirit that he would not die before he had seen the Lord's Messiah. Moved by the Spirit, he went into the temple courts. When the parents brought in the child Jesus to do for him what the custom of the Law required, Simeon took him in his arms and praised God, saying: "Sovereign Lord, as you have promised, you may now dismiss your servant in peace. For my eyes have seen your salvation, which you have prepared in the sight of all nations: a light for revelation to the Gentiles, and the glory of your people Israel.""*Luke 2:25-32 NIV

The story is self explanatory, Simeon has a purpose which was to prophesy about and pray for the coming of the messiah, with this job he was given the promise that he would see the answer to his prayer before he died. As a very old man, Simeon saw Jesus the promised salvation of the world. Only then did his spirit get ready to go back to heaven! He was now ready to die.

The third person was Anna, she also had a purpose and ministry of intercession, which also preserved her life. She lived to be very old and somehow God caused her to see Jesus as well.

*"There was also a prophet, Anna, the daughter of Penuel, of the tribe of Asher. She was very old; she had lived with her husband seven years after her marriage, and then was a widow until she was eighty-four. She never left the temple but worshiped night and day, fasting and praying. Coming up to them*

*at that very moment, she gave thanks to God and spoke about the child to all who were looking forward to the redemption of Jerusalem." Luke 2:36-38 NIV*

God brought together these two prophets to see the answer to their prayers. To one a clear promise was given that he will not die until he sees Jesus, but to the other, God simply led her to Jesus the answer to what she had been praying and fasting for!

Purpose, will preserve and elongate your life! May you not die before you fulfill your purpose! If God has promised you something may you not die until that promise has been fulfilled! You may be like Simeon who was clearly told that he would not die until he sees the promise fulfilled, but even if you don't have this clear promise, may you still pursue your purpose like Anna, who was equally preserved because she was faithfully serving God!

Serve God faithfully! Serve your generation faithfully and God will preserve your life!

### *Being at peace with all men*

We have extensively discussed the issue of being at peace with all men earlier in this book. This is very important so that you don't die with a weight of hate on your shoulders and a root of bitterness in your soul. We need to reach the end of our lives with no grudges or pain that imprisons our souls in the dungeons of hate and resentment.

But when is the end of our lives? We really don't know, it could be now, or sooner or later. So we ought to live as if today is our last day. If we live as if today is our last day then we better make sure that today we resolve all our pain. Or at least start working on it to make the most of the time we have left on this earth!

It means we really have no time to defer making peace with those who hurt us. Making peace is not always an easy thing. There are people whose job, it seems, is to make you uncomfortable, to taunt you and mock you for as long as they can. Such people can rarely be reasoned with, they will most likely not admit their wrong nor will they feel remorse. Such people must be forgiven even before they ask for it. It means we are the ones who benefit from forgiveness, we are the ones who are set free from the prison of hate and the shackles of pain and bitterness that bind our hearts!

These are such people as those who would reject Jesus and choose Barabas. These are such as those that would spit on Jesus, who would mock him and call him the King of the Jews! Who would place a thorny crown and press it deep into his head. These are those who would whip him with a rope that has metal hooks to rip his flesh apart. Those who would place a heavy cross on his severed and lacerated back and drive long rusty nails into his hands and feet. It is for these people that Jesus prayed *'Father, forgive them for they know not what they do!'*

Can you ask God to forgive those who taunt you! Those whose jobs, it seems, is to give you a tough time. These are those such as would stone Steven and for whom Steven would pray the exact same prayer as the Lord Jesus *'father forgive them and do not hold this sin against them.'*

Such people have no remorse, they could care less about whether or not you want to make peace. That's simply their way of life! Free yourself from their chains and pain over your life. Such people are not worth losing your peace over.

For those who can be won over do your best to win them over. Remember that your very prayers are hindered if there is no peace with your brother or even with your spouse. God commands us that if you have a sacrifice on the alter and you remember that your brother has something against you first reconcile yourself to your brother. So that your prayers can be heard.

Like Lazarus the taxman, you can make amends and you can offer restitution or restoration to those you have hurt. Like Jacob the twin, you can send gifts to you brother and confess your sin.

These weights are not worth carrying over into the next life and in fact can be impediments to eternal life and salvation. Where the hurts are too deep and beyond you. I would say 'hand them over to Jesus. Hand them over to God'. If you do so, God will minister to you and heal you both in this life and the one to come. He will put you in his comforting arms and in Abraham's bosom as he did to the poor man.

### *Be sure that you really don't believe in God*

We have people who don't believe in God and who think faith has no place in their lives.

People who believe this largely want to believe that they can escape accountability for their lives. They don't want to be accountable to anyone for their current actions or so they would like to believe. Contrary to this line of thinking the Bible says

*"Every human being is appointed to die once, and then to face God's judgment." Hebrews 9:27 TPT*

For people who do not believe in God, the Bible has a logical argument, look at the order in the universe, look at creation, don't be fooled that it's an accident or it is gradual perfection or evolution after millennia of trial and error, there is no order without an orchestrator. God is the orchestrator!

Everything on earth is fit for purpose and serves its own purpose hence contributing to the well being of the earth and life as we know it. Without an orchestrator there would be chaos and oblivion.

The reason why we don't want to believe in God is simply because we don't want to be subject to anyone! We want to be the captain of our souls. Well, I have a news flash, there are many things you are not and will never be in control of. One of them is your death, the second is what happens after your death. How you are handled is not up to you in any way. It is up to God the orchestrator of all things orderly in this universe.

But if we are to learn from simple laws of science the law of cause and effect means that our life has an impact on our world, on others and I dare say on the life beyond this world and it's short existence. So you better be sure that God is really dead and he does not exist, it's a question to which you cannot make a mistake on. It costs you your life, literally!

### *Be sure to escape hell*

The only time and opportunity we have to set right our spiritual destination is when we are alive. Once we die we only have to face judgement and we can no longer have an opportunity to set things right. This is seen in Jesus's story of the rich and poor man. Once the rich man was in hell there was nothing that could be done for him. However he could only plead for his brothers and asked Father Abraham to send Moses and the prophets to preach to them. This however is also not possible. All we have is now and the current preachers of the word. God has already made provision for us to get to heaven!

However, most of us procrastinate and think we will give our lives to God tomorrow or the next day or when situations are right. A perfect time will never come!

Some people think they need to be good enough in character before they can commit their lives to God, but if that were the case then we wouldn't need a Saviour! Because the truth is 'we can't save ourselves'. God wants you to come to him 'as you are' he will change you but you can't change yourself! You can't deliver yourself from bondage. Some feel rejected and ashamed to serve God because of their past, but God says 'even if your sins are as red as scarlet, they will become whiter than snow!'

Jesus says come unto me all you who labor and are heavy laden and I will give you rest! He says whoever comes to him he will in no way cast out. So, Jesus is ready to receive us just as we are.

The danger of indecisiveness is that we can run out of time while debating whether or not to commit our lives to God and to receive Jesus in our hearts as Lord and Savior! Unfortunately once we die the state in which we die, determines our eternal future!

*"and if the tree fall toward the south, or toward the north, in the place where the tree falleth, there it shall be."*

*Ecclesiastes 11:3 KJV*

Figuratively, our lives are trees which will one day fall. But the Bible says you can fall either pointing toward the north, or the south and in whatever direction you fall, there you will lie!

Friends if you die in Christ, your spirit is pointed heavenward. If you die in sin your spirit is pointed toward hell and eternal damnation!

But there is hope, you can change your indecisiveness and commit your life to God.

*"Anyone who is among the living has hope —even a live dog is better off than a dead lion!" Ecclesiastes 9:4 NIV*

The key to your hope is that you are still alive, you have this book in your hands and it means you still have breath in your body! And as long as you are alive, there is hope, you can ask Jesus to come into your heart right now, you can ask him to be Lord and Saviour, you can confess with your mouth that he is Lord, that he died for your sins and rose again from the grave to save you!

It does not matter how many mistakes you have made in the past. It does not matter if you did not start well, because you can end well! All that matters is that you end well!

*"The end of a matter is better than its beginning, and patience is better than pride." Ecclesiastes 7:8 NIV*

So don't listen to those who mock you and those that belittle you, of who you were in the past or who you are now, what matters is who you will become in Jesus!

You don't have to wait any longer because as long as it is today, you can be saved, today, and not tomorrow, is the day of your salvation.

*"As has just been said: "Today, if you hear his voice, do not harden your hearts as you did in the rebellion.""*

*Hebrews 3:15 NIV*

As long as it is today and as long as you are alive you have hope. It doesn't matter how you look at yourself, you might think of yourself as a dog, the lowest of all! But to you Jesus says exactly what he said to the woman caught in adultery,

'I do not condemn you, but go and sin no more'.

# 14

# Seeing transition through the lens of God's love

Transition must be seen through the lens of God's love! But how can it be that something as painful as death can be as a result of God's love? There are several reasons and hopefully after we look at each one we will see that indeed God ultimately loves us in spite of the existence of death.

### *Protection from the tree of life*

In the book of Genesis the age old story is told of how Adam sinned by eating from the tree of the knowledge of good and evil. God warned Adam that if he eats from that tree he would 'surely die'.

*"And the Lord God commanded the man, "You are free to eat from any tree in the garden; but you must not eat from the tree of the knowledge of good and evil, for when you eat from it you will certainly die."" Genesis 2:16-17 NIV*

As we know however, Adam disobeyed and something else followed,

*"And the Lord God said, "The man has now become like one of us, knowing good and evil. He must not be allowed to reach out his hand and take also from*

*the tree of life and eat, and live forever." So the Lord God banished him from the Garden of Eden to work the ground from which he had been taken. After he drove the man out, he placed on the east side of the Garden of Eden cherubim and a flaming sword flashing back and forth to guard the way to the tree of life." Genesis 3:22-24 NIV*

What we see in these passages of scripture is that God deliberately prevented man from eating of the tree of life. The reason is simple, God did not want Adam to live forever in his sinful state! If this were to happen there would be no opportunity to literally purify his fallen spirit and fallen body. God, instead, in his loving kindness sought to deliver man from the trap of sin by making a plan of salvation. This plan would first of all deal with the disobedient and fallen heart of man. Once his heart is cleansed and delivered, he could then be given a new body that would live forever. In this redeemed state, he can freely live forever in the presence of God knowing that his corruption of evil has been healed and cleansed.

Can you imagine all the evil that has so far happened in this world! All the wars, all the genocides, the holocaust, racism, rape, and all types of evil! Can you imagine the wickedness in the time of Noah that led to a flood on the whole earth, or can you imagine the evil inhabitants of Sodom and Gomorrah? Can you imagine if the perpetrators of all these evils lived for ever? Wow! That would be terrible isn't it? The world would have been such a terrible, wicked and evil place! All this because a seed of disobedience was planted in the heart of Adam and Eve!

God did not want such a world filled with wickedness and unimaginable evil. He had to ensure that Adam does not access the tree of life or he would live forever. God's problem was not the fact that he would live forever, rather his problem was that man would live in sin forever!

So from this perspective death is God's way of protecting Adam and his children from the eternal clutch of a 'sinful and wicked immortality'. Praise God for that!

When Jesus comes again at the rapture he will recreate and resurrect our bodies and reunite them with our souls that are in heaven! That's why the Bible says that even our current bodies are groaning for deliverance from decay and the power of sin!

*"For we know that all creation has been groaning as in the pains of childbirth right up to the present time. And we believers also groan, even though we have the Holy Spirit within us as a foretaste of future glory, for we long for our bodies to be released from sin and suffering. We, too, wait with eager hope for the day when God will give us our full rights as his adopted children, including the new bodies he has promised us."*

*Romans 8:22-23 NLT*

*"And not only this, but we too, who have the first fruits of the Spirit [a joyful indication of the blessings to come], even we groan inwardly, as we wait eagerly for [the sign of] our adoption as sons—the redemption and transformation of our body [at the resurrection]." Romans 8:23 AMP*

So the first thing we see is that it was necessary for man to die because of sin. Living in an eternally sinful state is not God's loving idea for his children. It was necessary that he gives us more glorious bodies at the resurrection! And for this to happen these bodies must die!

## *God's sovereignty*

Sometimes we all wonder why bad things happen to God's people. We cannot answer every question but we know that generally corruption and evil and wickedness came into the word as a result of sin.

We also know that even the whole creation is crying out to be delivered from this corruption. And one day this will happen. In this imperfect world, God still works to fulfill his purposes for our lives and sometimes he does things that we cannot understand.

For example Job could not understand why and how he lost his animals and servants to a raid of attackers. He also lost his 10 children at one go!

It is normal therefore to be angry at God and think he is good for nothing. That he is actually evil and unkind. But God is sovereign and he has his own purposes and reasons. He is a king who cannot be questioned! He answers to no one and indeed King Solomon emphasizes this fact.

*"For the king's word hath power; and who may say unto him, What doest thou?" Ecclesiastes 8:4 ASV*

*For the word of the king is supreme, and who may say to him, "What are you doing?" Ecclesiastes 8:4 ESV*

*Our God is in heaven he does whatever pleases him Psalm 115:3*

Because Job realized this he was able to guide his wife who despaired and sought to curse God in her anger. He told her that God is the one who gives and he is the one who takes away, we came with nothing in this world and we will go back with nothing.

All we need to do is to continue trusting him with the little truth that we know and that has been revealed to us.

*"The secret things belong to the LORD our God, but the things that are revealed belong to us and to our children forever, that we may do all the words of this law. Deuteronomy 29:29*

We also need to trust that he works all things for our good,

*The righteous man perishes, and no one lays it to heart;*

*devout men are taken away, while no one understands.*

*For the righteous man is taken away from calamity; he enters into peace; they rest in their beds who walk in their uprightness.*

*Isaiah 57:1-2*

*And we know that for those who love God all things work together for good, for those who are called according to his purpose. Romans 8:28*

When we realize the supremacy of God we come to terms with certain things. Firstly, that God is supreme, he is in heaven and therefore his ways are much much higher than our ways. If his ways are much higher we can only understand in part. Therefore we sometimes have to leave the secret things to God and God alone! But in all these things, we know that he is a God of love, sometimes death happens to take us away from future calamity and that all in all, God makes everything work for our good!

### *Jesus died too*

Sometimes we hear the words 'you're not the only one who is going through what your going through'. To be honest it's not the best comfort you can have because it does not immediately solve your current problem. At least that's how I feel. However, it does encourage you that if others have experienced what you are experiencing and they overcame, then you too can overcome. I think this is what we see here but more than that, Jesus did not simply die as all of us do, but he actually died for us in the sense that he experienced it in order to help us go through it! Only when you know how challenging something is can you help others go through what you have gone through.

*"Therefore, since [these His] children share in flesh and blood [the physical nature of mankind], He Himself in a similar manner also shared in the same [physical nature, but without sin], so that through [experiencing] death He might make powerless (ineffective, impotent) him who had the power of death—that is, the devil— and [that He] might free all those who through [the haunting] fear of death were held in slavery throughout their lives." Hebrews 2:14-15 AMP*

This passage says something profound. Jesus does not want you and I to fear death! Imagine that? Living without fearing death? Wow that's another level of faith in God and his power. It is possible because firstly, Jesus died as well! Secondly, in his death he overcame the devil who 'had' power over death. It means that now Jesus has the power over death! Isn't that comforting? I think it is. So Jesus does not want you and I to be haunted by death! Or even the thought of death! No! Not at all!

If you were held in slavery to the fear and haunting of death, Jesus has come to set you free! You are free from this fear! Because Jesus died for you! He disarmed the devil and death is powerless before him!

The passage continues by saying

*"For, as we all know, He (Christ) does not take hold of [the fallen] angels [to give them a helping hand], but He does take hold of [the fallen] descendants of Abraham [extending to them His hand of deliverance]. Therefore, it was essential that He had to be made like His brothers (mankind) in every respect,*

*so that He might [by experience] become a merciful and faithful High Priest in things related to God, to make atonement (propitiation) for the people's sins [thereby wiping away the sin, satisfying divine justice, and providing a way of reconciliation between God and mankind]. Because He Himself [in His humanity] has suffered in being tempted, He is able to help and provide immediate assistance to those who are being tempted and exposed to suffering." Hebrews 2:16-18 AMP*

This passage emphasizes the fact that because Jesus became one of us he understands our fears and our weaknesses. This includes our fear of death! He knows what it means to be tempted, he knows what it means to lose and mourn a loved one, because he lost his own father when he was a young man, yes, Jesus knows what it means to mourn. He did not only mourn his father but also his friend Lazarus, he knows what it means for people to die, he sees the sorrow of families who lose loved ones, he saw this sorrow in the story of the young man on his way to burial or the daughter of Jairus, a synagogue official, he saw the anguish of the mourners, he even saw the anguish of his mother who saw him hang on the cross. And eventually he himself experienced the pangs and the pain of death!

Friends Jesus did not just die for our sin! Jesus died to experience death and help us through it!

*"What we do see is Jesus, who for a little while was given a position "a little lower than the angels"; and because he suffered death for us, he is now "crowned with glory and honor." Yes, by God's grace,* ***Jesus tasted death for everyone."*** *Hebrews 2:9 NLT*

### *Jesus is our way through death*

Jesus is many things to the believer. In John 19 he describes himself as the good shepherd and Peter describes him as the Shepherd and Overseer of our souls! (1 Pet 2:25)

Such a shepherd will not leave you in death! Actually he will lead you and guide you!

Jesus is also the door of the sheep! And in John 14:1-6 he tells his disciples *that I am the way to the father! I am the only way!*

Though we sleep the sleep of death this only happens to our bodies! Our spirits walk in the light of our Shepherd Jesus Christ, Jesus boldly proclaims this and says

*" I am the Light of the world. He who follows Me will not walk in the darkness, but will have the Light of life." John 8:12 AMP*

So even in death we walk in light! While our bodies sleep our spirits are alive and walking in the light of life! Jesus is our light and we walk in his light!

Death for the believer is not the same experience as death for the sinner or unbeliever! For the unbeliever death is banishment from God's presence just as Adam was banished. It is also being separated just as Jesus was separated from God. Jesus was separated from the presence of his father and he lamented that God had forsaken him and indeed the darkness of sin and death filled all the earth! But Jesus' death made him bear that punishment on our behalf so that we are never separated from God again!

In fact in Jesus we are forever alive! And indeed Jesus demonstrates this by saying God is not a God of the dead! No he is a God of the living, he calls himself the God of Abraham, Isaac and Jacob, because these patriarchs are still alive in his presence! (That's why Elijah and Moses appeared to Jesus and talked to him on the mount of the transfiguration (Math 17:1-3) that's why in Luke 16 we see father Abraham, comforting the poor man in his bosom! Friends those who die in Christ are not lost! They are not dead! They are alive and well!

Never despair, never ever despair for those who died believing in God!

For us believers, death is a process of taking off our tent. It is the putting aside of our tent which Peter says he will shortly lay it aside! 2 Cor 5:1, 2 Pet 1:13-14. This body is a cloak that we have been clothed with and we will all put it away!

We are not alone when we die, Jesus promises to welcome us and come and take us. He sends us his angels who carry us into heaven immediately. Unlike unbelievers who go to a waiting place called Sheol or Hades as they wait their judgement in torment, we go to heaven to be with Jesus in paradise. Luke 16:19-23.

In fact, all in all death is gain for the believer! It is gain because we go to be with Jesus for eternity!

*"For to me, to live is Christ [He is my source of joy, my reason to live] and to die is gain [for I will be with Him in eternity]." Philippians 1:21 AMP*

### ***God is never taken by surprise !***

The shock that sometimes overtakes us in loss can be quite overwhelming. We easily despair because of the pain and confusion. But God says he is not taken by surprise! God takes care of even the minutest details so much so that he cannot be unconcerned about what happens to his children. We should know that God has even numbered your individual hairs and no single bird dies without God knowing and allowing it. If God knows this then we should not be afraid at all regarding the future!

*"What is the price of two sparrows—one copper coin? But not a single sparrow can fall to the ground without your Father knowing it. And the very hairs on your head are all numbered. So don't be afraid; you are more valuable to God than a whole flock of sparrows." Matthew 10:29-31*

*Death will be destroyed!*

Death is causing havoc now but the day is surely coming when it will be destroyed and utterly so!

*"Then death and Hades [the realm of the dead] were thrown into the lake of fire. This is the second death, the lake of fire [the eternal separation from God]." Revelation 20:14 AMP*

It is comforting to know that even death will be destroyed! So don't fear! God has you sorted!

If you are not a follower of Jesus however, a terrifying fate awaits you,

*"And if anyone's name was not found written in the Book of Life, he was hurled into the lake of fire." Revelation 20:15 AMP*

May this not be your portion, may you make things right with God today! While you still have breath!

### *We will be comforted*

Our transition into heaven is the beginning of God's healing of all our pain and sufferings and our sorrows shall flee away!

*"Therefore the redeemed of the Lord shall return, and come with singing unto Zion; and everlasting joy shall be upon their head: they shall obtain gladness and joy; and sorrow and mourning shall flee away." Isaiah 51:11 KJV*

Our tears will be wiped away completely

*"And God shall wipe away all tears from their eyes; and there shall be no more death, neither sorrow, nor crying, neither shall there be any more pain: for the former things are passed away."*

*Revelation 21:4 KJV*

*"And it came to pass, that the beggar died, and that he was carried away by the angels into Abraham's bosom: and the rich man also died, and was buried." Luke 16:22 ASV*

*"Blessed are the poor in spirit: for theirs is the kingdom of heaven. Blessed are they that mourn: for they shall be comforted.*

*Blessed are the merciful: for they shall obtain mercy. Blessed are the pure in heart: for they shall see God.*

*Blessed are they that have been persecuted for righteousness' sake: for theirs is the kingdom of heaven. Blessed are ye when men shall reproach you, and persecute you, and say all manner of evil against you falsely, for my sake. Rejoice, and be exceeding glad: for great is your reward in heaven: for so persecuted they the prophets that were before you." Matthew 5:3-4, 7-8, 10-12 ASV*

Being received in heaven means we are receiving comfort and healing from all our earthly pain. It's a time to be comforted and to receive our reward!

### *We are covered by the love of God!*

All in all when we look at what God has done we see his love all over! He knows that death is tough but he has made provision for us through Jesus Christ! Jesus is our everything! He is our light, our shepherd, our door, and our way to the Father!

He even experienced death on our behalf so he is able to help us and comfort us through it.

God gives us the presence of the Holy Spirit through your life and even in death! His presence is inescapable in life and in death!

*"Where can I go from Your Spirit? Or where can I flee from Your presence? If I ascend to heaven, You are there; If I make my bed in Sheol (the nether world, the place of the dead), behold, You are there." Psalms 139:7-8 AMP*

Before the resurrection of Jesus all spirits of men were in a place called Sheol. And even there God was present with his righteous people. But with Jesus we have a straight highway into heaven! When Jesus came he took the souls of all the righteous into heaven' so don't be afraid! Either in death or in life Jesus is with you! God is with you!

In fact he emphasizes that nothing, completely nothing can separate us from the love of God in Christ Jesus!

*"For I am convinced that neither death nor life, neither angels nor demons, neither the present nor the future, nor any powers, neither height nor depth, nor anything else in all creation, will be able to separate us from the love of God that is in Christ Jesus our Lord." Romans 8:38-39 NIV*

*Even in trouble and persecution God loves you,*
*In life God loves you!*
*In death God loves you!*
*You cannot escape his presence!*
*You cannot escape his love!*

Then what is the conclusion of this matter, if you are a believer, you must not despair!, You must not fear! You must see death through the lens of God's love!

# 15

# The door to heaven

***A prayer for those who want to make heaven their home***

*Dear Jesus,*

*You have said that "I am the way, the truth and the life".*

*Today I choose to believe that indeed you are the way to heaven, the way to my heavenly father, you are the truth of the world and you are my life!*

*I believe you have gone to heaven to prepare a place for me*

*To prepare room for me in your father's house*

*You have said "there are many rooms in my father's house"*

*and "where I am going you will be also."*

*Jesus I want to go to heaven I want to come home after this life*

*I want to come to my father in heaven!*

*Therefore I ask for the forgiveness of my sins through*

*The shed blood of Jesus as the only atonement for my sin*

*I confess with my mouth that Jesus you are the Lord of my life and I receive you as my personal savior*

*I believe that you rose again from the dead*

*I thank you that you have forgiven my sin and written my name in the book of life*

*In Jesus name I have prayed...*

*Amen*

*Name* ............................................ *Date* ............................................

# References

The following are key references for the miracles of Elijah and Elisha.

**Miracles in the Career of Elijah**

1. Causing the rain the cease for 3 1/2 years (1Ki 17:1)
2. Being fed by the ravens (1Ki 17:4)
3. Miracle of the barrel of meal and cruse of oil (1Ki 17:14)
4. Resurrection of the widow's son (1Ki 17:22)
5. Calling of fire from heaven on the altar (1Ki 18:38)
6. Causing it to rain (1Ki 18:45)
7. Prophecy that Ahab's sons would all be destroyed (1Ki 21:22)
8. Prophecy that Jezebel would be eaten by dogs (1Ki 21:23)
9. Prophecy that Ahaziah would die of his illness (2Ki 1:4)
10. Calling fire from heaven upon the first 50 soldiers (2Ki 1:10)
11. Calling fire from heaven upon the second 50 soldiers (2Ki 1:12)
12. Parting of the Jordan (2Ki 2:8)
13. 1Prophecy that Elisha should have a double portion of his spirit (2Ki 2:10)
14. Being caught up to heaven in a whirlwind (2Ki 2:11)

# References

**Miracles in the Career of Elisha:**

1. Parting of the Jordan (2Ki 2:14)
2. Healing of the waters (2Ki 2:21)
3. Curse of the she bears (2Ki 2:24)
4. Filling of the valley with water (2Ki 3:17)
5. Deception of the Moabites with the valley of blood (2Ki 3:22)
6. Miracle of the vessels of oil (2Ki 4:4)
7. Prophecy that the Shunammite woman would have a son (2Ki 4:16)
8. Resurrection of the Shunammite's son (2Ki 4:34)
9. Healing of the gourds (2Ki 4:41)
10. Miracle of the bread (2Ki 4:43)
11. Healing of Naaman (2Ki 5:14)
12. Perception of Gehazi's transgression (2Ki 5:26)
13. Cursing Gehazi with leprosy (2Ki 5:27)
14. Floating of the axe head (2Ki 6:6)
15. Prophecy of the Syrian battle plans (2Ki 6:9)
16. Vision of the chariots (2Ki 6:17)
17. Smiting the Syrian army with blindness (2Ki 6:18)
18. Restoring the sight of the Syrian army (2Ki 6:20)
19. Prophecy of the end of the great famine (2Ki 7:1)
20. Prophecy that the scoffing nobleman would see, but not partake of, the abundance (2Ki 7:2)
21. Deception of the Syrians with the sound of chariots (2Ki 7:6)
22. Prophecy of the seven-year famine (2Ki 8:1)
23. Prophecy of Benhadad's untimely death (2Ki 8:10)
24. Prophecy of Hazael's cruelty to Israel (2Ki 8:12)
25. Prophecy that Jehu would smite the house of Ahab (2Ki 9:7)
26. Prophecy that Joash would smite the Syrians at Aphek (2Ki 13:17)

27. Prophecy that Joash would smite Syria thrice but not consume it (2Ki 13:19)
28. Resurrection of the man touched by his bones (2Ki 13:21)

The following scripture references are assigned the related meanings

| | |
|---|---|
| NKJV | New King James Version |
| AMP | Amplified version |
| ESV | English Standard version |
| NLT | New Living Translation |
| NIV | New international Version |

Moffat David is a father of two lovely kids, Sean and Aretha. He is a Fellow Chartered Accountant and licenced auditor and an IT governance professional. He is an Associate Director of PricewaterhouseCoopers in his home country. He is also the Vice President and Board Member of his national accountancy body and enjoys serving as a lay member of his local church.

www.ingramcontent.com/pod-product-compliance
Ingram Content Group UK Ltd.
Pitfield, Milton Keynes, MK11 3LW, UK
UKHW041830200726
13854UKWH00002BA/913

9 789990 809312